From the library of

Natalie Rittenhouse

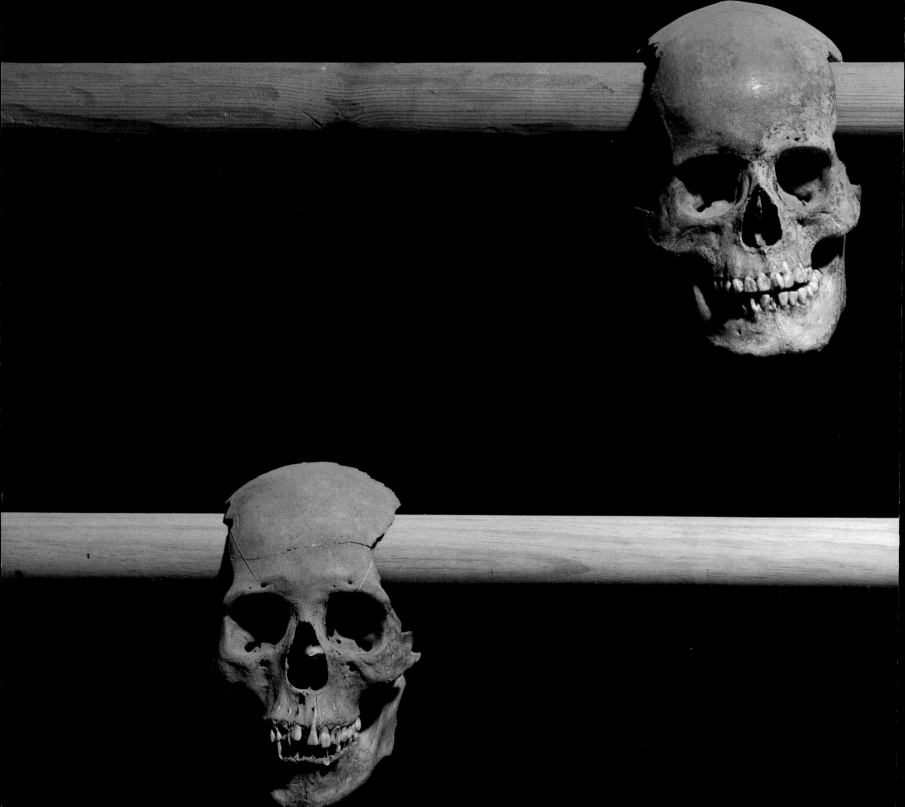

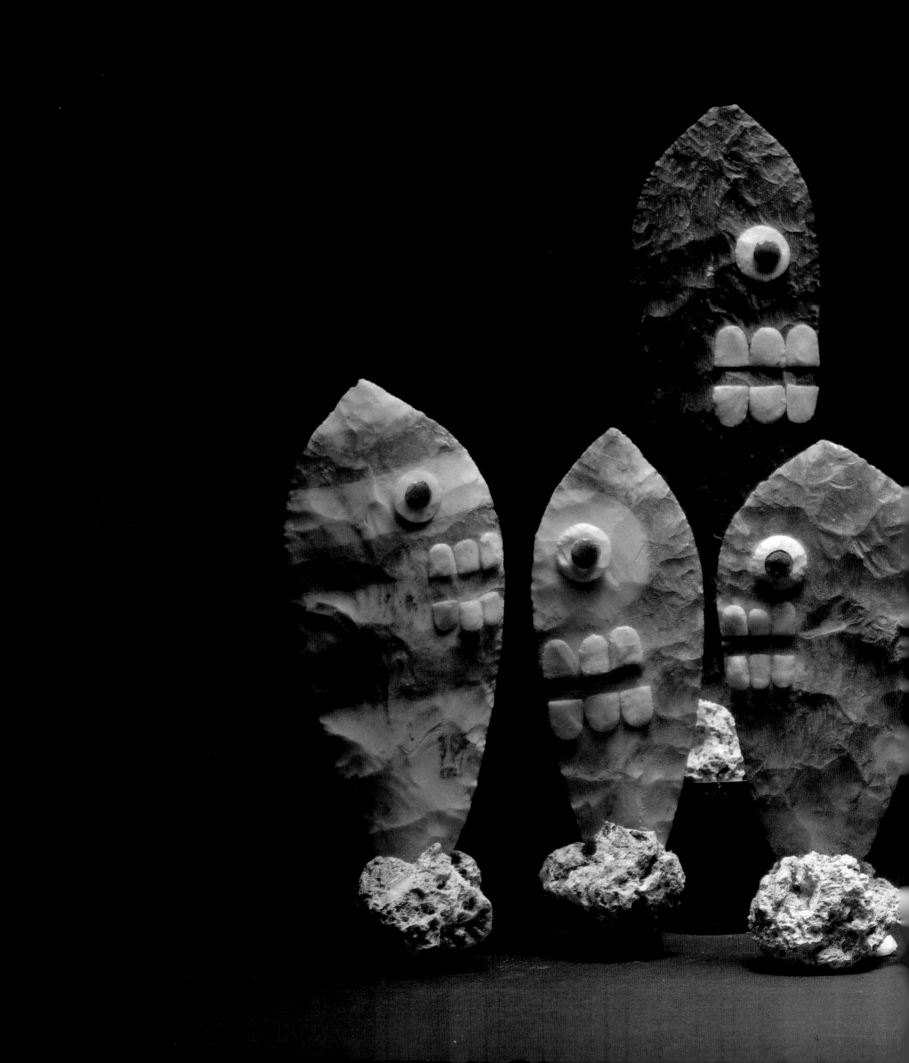

p. 1:

Cuauhxicalli eagle; *Basalt sculpture (139 x 82 x 72 cm). Mexica culture.*

p. 2 and 3:

Skulls from Tzompantli altar. *Mexica culture.*

p. 4 and 5:

Group of Tecpatl ceremonial knives; *Silex, copal base with shell inscrustations. Mexica culture.*

p. 6 and 7:

Tubular figures; *Polychromed green stone. Tradition widespread throughout central and southern portions of Mesoamerica.*

p. 8:

Teotihuacan mask; *Green stone with incrustations of shell and obsidian (21.5 x 21.2 cm).*
Teotihuacan culture.

TREASURES OF THE GREAT TEMPLE

AL TI
PUBLISHING

Acknowledgments

We wish to thank the National Institute of
Anthropology and History (Instituto Nacional de Antropología e Historia), The National Council for Arts and Culture (Conse-
jo Nacional Para la Cultura y las Artes) and
Fomento Cultural Banamex, A.C. for their
support and assistance in the production of
this book. We are also grateful to the per-
sonnel of the Museum of the Templo Mayor
for their enthusiastic cooperation.

Published by: Alti Publishing
            4180 La Jolla Village Drive Suite 250
            La Jolla California 92037

Produced by: Alfonso Bullé Goyri & Martín Jon García-Urtiaga
Design by: Ana Elena Pérez
Assistant Editor: Michael Calderwood
Translated by: Richard Lindley
Assistant to Mr. Zabé: Reynaldo Izquierdo

The Spanish language first edition was published by
Fomento Cultural Banamex A.C. in 1988 under the title:
Obras Maestras del Templo Mayor.

Published in the United States of America.

Library of Congress catalog card number 89 — 081881

ISBN 0-9625399-6-1

Printed in Japan by Toppan Printing Company

TREASURES OF THE GREAT TEMPLE

TEXT
EDUARDO MATOS MOCTEZUMA

PHOTOGRAPHY
MICHEL ZABÉ

PRODUCED BY
FUNDACIÓN UNIVERSO VEINTIUNO, A.C.

CONTENTS

INTRODUCTION   17

DEATH OF THE GODS   19

RESURRECTION OF THE GODS   25

SYMBOLISM OF THE GREAT TEMPLE   31

BURIED STONES   37

MUSEUM OF THE GREAT TEMPLE   61

HUITZILOPOCHTLI: WAR AND DEATH   63

TRIBUTE-PAYING REGIONS   83

WARRIOR GRANDEUR   107

LEGEND OF COYOLXAUHQUI   122

TLALOC: WATER AND LIFE   127

FAUNA OF THE GREAT TEMPLE   147

CONQUEST   171

MAP OF ARCHEOLOGICAL SITE   176

ANNOTATED BIBLIOGRAPHY   178

Numeral "2 Cane"; Stone table (97 x 52 x 10 cm). Mexica culture.

INTRODUCTION

The archeologist has it within his power to give life to the world of inanimate objects. He digs into the earth, goes deep into time, and comes face to face with the gods and peoples of the past. In 1978 it was my privilege once more to transcend the barriers of time and penetrate into the heart of a city, the city of Mexico.

The place now occupied by this enormous metropolis was once home to many ancient cities. One of them was Cuicuilco, which flourished around 600 B.C. A series of urban centers succeeded one another in its place until the year 1325 A.D., when the Aztecs founded the city of Tenochtitlan on an island in the middle of Lake Texcoco in the Valley of Mexico. Tenochtitlan grew and developed for almost 200 years until it was destroyed by the Spaniards in 1521. Its ruins then became the foundation for the colonial city which has become the present capital of Mexico.

Today it is possible to view the remains of the Templo Mayor, the Great Temple of the Aztecs. It was an honor to be one of those who spent five years excavating the site with great care until we arrived at the center of the ancient Aztec city. A whole team of archeologists and other specialists made this great discovery possible. The environs of the Templo Mayor and its offerings were uncovered and are now on public display.

Michel Zabé's magnificent photographs reveal the very essence of these finds. The buildings, the sculptures, the masks—in short, everything that was buried here for five hundred years has been brought into the light by the wonderful time machine of Archeology.

All this will come to life as you turn the pages of this book...

Eduardo Matos Moctezuma

Anthropomorphic male figure; Green stone with incrustations of pyrite, decorated in red and white (23.3 x 10 x 5 cm). Guerrero area culture.

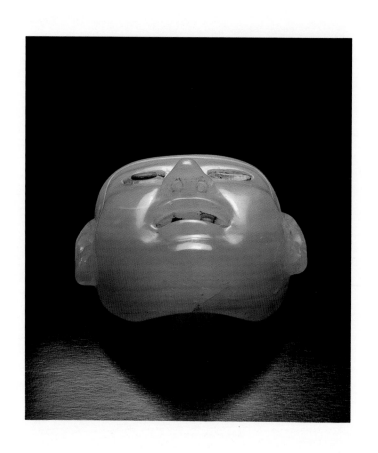

18

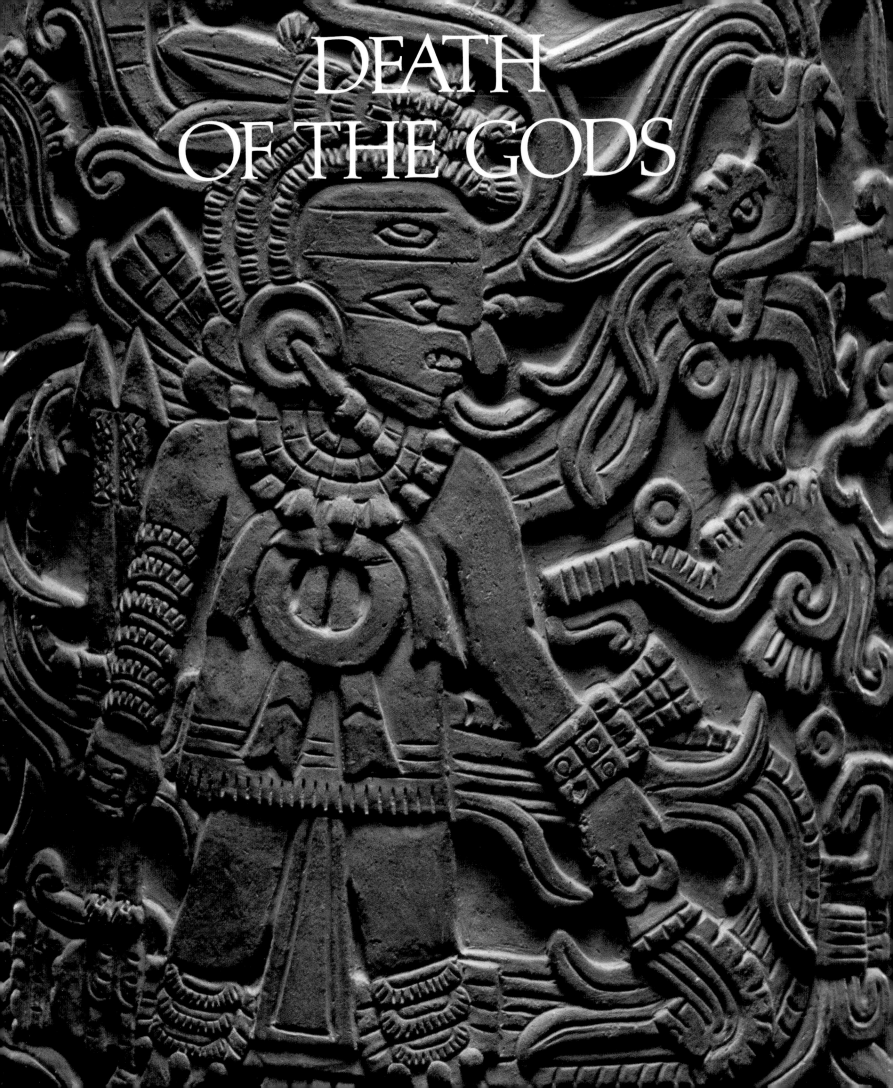

DEATH
OF THE GODS

Glasgow Manuscript; *Description of the City and Province of Tlaxcala.*

It is August 13, 1521. Death rules everywhere in Tenochtitlan, capital of the Aztec empire. For three months, the city has been under siege. The bridges have been destroyed, the causeways show the ravages of combat. Day after day the struggle has gone on without respite. The drinking water that once flowed from Chapultepec has been cut off, and the normal routes of supply along the great causeways that connect the city with dry land are blocked.

On the water the struggle is no less intense. Fleets of canoes full of Mexica warriors attack the Spanish contingents and their allies again and again, and the latter strive to avenge the many affronts they have suffered at the hands of the arrogant Mexicas. A large part of the population of Tenochtitlan has sought refuge in Tlatelolco, which has become the center of native resistance. To an invitation to surrender, the last Mexica *Tlatoani*, the Speaker (or ruler), replies:

Well, since you wish it so, then carefully husband the maize and provisions we have, and let us all die fighting. Henceforward let no one dare to ask me for peace, for if anyone does, I will have him slain.

The fighting continues, and the moment comes when further resistance is useless. Cuauhtémoc knows this. Together with some of his official retinue and a number of women, he sails for dry land. The Spaniards learn of this maneuver and one of their brigantines accosts the party before they reach their destination. Cuauhtémoc and his followers are detained and taken immediately to Cortés. This encounter between the two great enemy chiefs will reveal the complete lack of understanding that beset two very different cultures, two radically different ways of thinking. Thus, when the Aztec *Tlatoani* stands before Cortés, he tells him:

Lord Malinche, I have done my duty in defense of my city. There is nothing more I can do. Hence, as I am forced to come before you a prisoner of your power, take the dagger you wear at your side and kill me with it at once.

This speech, recorded by Bernal Díaz del Castillo as it was spoken in Nahuatl by Cuauhtémoc and translated for Cortés, was not understood in its full significance. What the young *Tlatoani* meant is this: as a prisoner of war he was entitled to be sacrificed according to the custom of his tribe so that, as a warrior, he might accompany the sun in its sweep across the sky, for this was the proper fate of warriors killed in combat or taken prisoner for the sacrifice. He was not asking for pardon, but for the death a warrior deserves.

Cortés, however, does not understand him; instead, in good "Christian" manner, he forgives him. The young prisoner desires death —the death to which his customs entitle him— far more than the extended life to which he is condemned. Here are two diametrically opposed intentions, two distinct ways of thinking and being. This lack of understanding will determine the future destiny of the two antagonists: the Indian, who must submit to exploitation, and the Spaniard, his inquisitor and lord.

With the military conquest of the city thus consummated, an even more arduous struggle began for ideological conquest through the vehicle of a Church that served the conquerors' purposes. Destruction of the Indians' city and temples was systematic. Fray Toribio de Benavente, also known as Motolinía, compared it to the seventh plague of Egypt. Here are the words used by the monk in his *Memoriales*:

The seventh plague [was] the construction of the great city of Mexico, in which more people labored in the first years than in the construction of the temple of Jerusalem during the reign of Solomon, for so many were those who worked at this task, or who came to bring materials or provisions and tribute to the Spaniards and to those who were engaged in the public works, that one could hardly force his way along the streets and causeways, although they are quite broad. And at the work sites, some were stricken by beams, others fell from heights, and still others fell under the buildings that were being razed in one place in order to be rebuilt in another.

How terrible it must have been for the conquered Indians to have to destroy their own gods and temples and use the very rubble to raise up new ones! Ideological resistance was not long in making itself felt. Motolinía also tells how the recently subjugated Indians tried to continue paying homage to their gods by hiding them behind the new Christian altars:

Then they saw that they had kept some images at their altars together with their

demons and idols; and in other places the image in view and the idol hidden either behind a drape or behind the wall, or within the altar, and so they removed them, as many as they could find, telling them that if they wanted to have images of God or Saint Mary, they must build them a church.

We also know how the Indians chose a certain type of sculpture that represented Tlaltecuhtli, the earth god who devoured all corpses, and reworked it into the base of a column so that the figure of the god was facing down against the earth, thus avoiding the suspicions of the monks, who would surely have insisted that the figure of the idol remain unseen. "Do not worry, your grace," the Indian must have replied, "this figure is going to be underneath."

In this way the good priest was appeased, while the Indians succeeded in their purpose of preserving the figure of Tlaltecuhtli, for the rightful position of this god was precisely facedown and unseen. Here was something the Western mind could not understand. For the Westerner, if something is carefully wrought it must surely be intended for viewing, an idea which had no correspondence in the prehispanic world.

As the struggle between these two cultures continued and the Spaniards penetrated ever deeper, the conquistadors strove to erase the world of the native American altogether. All that was considered the work of the devil was destroyed and the way made straight for the work of the angels.

This was in fact one of Cortés's driving motives: to leave no trace of that which constituted the holy places of the Mexica. There is no doubt that he was aware of the importance to the Mexicas' cosmology of the ceremonial center and the Templo Mayor. The latter signified the *Center of the Universe*, the navel of the world, the home of the supreme duality, from which one could as well ascend the heavens to *Omeyocan* or descend to the world of the dead and find oneself face to face with Death. From the temple rayed out the four directions of the world, each governed by its own god, its own color, its own symbol. It was, as well, the place where myths came to life in an eternal becoming, where sacrifice and death took place daily in order to sustain the life of the sun and of man who, impotent, has given creation into the hands of the gods.

All of this would be destroyed. Of the Templo Mayor in its last architectural phase not one stone would remain over another. And out of the destruction of the Templo Mayor would emerge the Christian cathedral. With that unequal confrontation in Tlatelolco began the death of the ancient gods.

It all began on that fateful day of August 13, 1521.

RESURRECTION OF THE GODS

August 13, 1790, marks the date of the discovery at the Plaza de Armas (now the Zócalo) in Mexico City of the monumental statue of the earth goddess Coatlicue. A few months later, on December 17 of the same year, another discovery only a few meters away from the resting place of the Mother of the Gods also stirred the imagination of the late Spanish colonials. This time it was the *Piedra del Sol*, the Sun Stone, commonly known as the Aztec Calendar. The leveling of the Plaza, a project ordered by the Viceroy Conde de Revillagigedo, had borne unexpected fruit—an encounter with a world that three centuries earlier was cast down by evangelical Spaniards.

What was the significance of this coincidence of dates: August 13, 1521, and August 13, l790? Did the ancient gods resurface in order to assume their rightful place in history with respect to that first August 13 in Tlatelolco? A question for the gods, say the believers. A simple coincidence, say the scientists. But some coincidences truly give pause for thought.

Another coincidence involving the Templo Mayor concerns Alonso de Avila Alvarado, son of a conquistador. Let us go back to 1566, when the young Don Alonso is living in a mansion built by his father on a plot of land granted to him by Don Hernán Cortés on a site located immediately above the ruins of the Templo Mayor. Don Alonso and his brother Gil are known throughout New Spain for their parties and soirees. Their power is evident and soon, together with other sons of conquerors (among their number is Don Martín, son of Don Hernán Cortés) they begin to conspire against the Spanish Crown. They claim that their fathers sired them to conquer these lands, that it is unjust to force them to render money and tribute to Spain considering the cost they have already paid to win the New World.

The rebellion takes shape and these young men feel ever more intensely that justice is on their side, to such an extent that the conspiracy is already common knowledge in every corner of the colonial capital. The authorities are not unaware of what is being planned and they act without delay. On June 16, 1566, they call the young Marqués del Valle, Don Martín Cortés, before the Audiencia, under the pretext that certain news has arrived from the royal capital of which he must be informed. Once they are assembled in the presence of the judges, the president of the Audiencia, Señor Ceynos, addresses Don Martín and says:

"Marqués, consider yourself a prisoner of the King."

"Why am I made prisoner?", he answers in surprise.

"For treason against His Majesty."

"You lie! I am no traitor, nor are any of my lineage."

In the end Don Martín was forced to surrender. At the same moment, the Avila brothers and many other conspirators, including the Dean Chico de Molina, were also being arrested. A summary trial was held and a few days later, to the mortification of New Spain's most powerful families and to the utter stupefaction of the conspirators themselves, they were declared guilty of treason against the Crown. Sentence was handed down on August 3 of the same year (1566). Those most severely affected, for they lost their life and all their possessions, were Don Alonso and Don Gil. Both were sentenced to decapitation in the Plaza Mayor. Their houses were ordered razed to the foundation and their land sewn with salt. An accusatory inscription in stone was posted at the site. It can still be seen today, embedded in a wall across the street from the ruins of the Templo Mayor, at the exact location where Coyolxauhqui was found, in the very heart of Mexico City. The inscription reads:

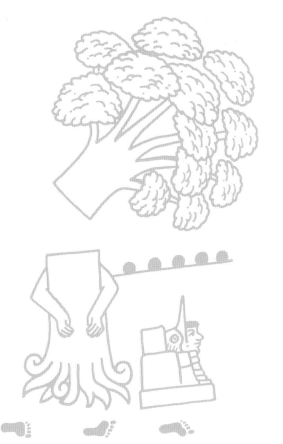

These buildings belonged to Al[onso] de Avila Alvarado, resident of this City of Mexico, who was condemned to death as a traitor. The sentence was executed on his person in the public square of this city, and the structures which were the principal buildings of his residence were ordered torn down. Year of 15[ ] (probably the same year of 1566).

The coincidence is stunning. Those who had helped to destroy the Templo Mayor, who no doubt used the very stones of the principal Mexica temple to build their mansions, now saw their homes destroyed. And here only two meters below the ground lay Coyolxauhqui—the goddess who, like those young rebels who lived above the ruins of the Templo Mayor, was beheaded.

But let us return to the year 1790. The Mexica monuments uncovered during the remodeling of the Plaza de Armas were apparently seen with fresh eyes, not the eyes of conquest. Instead of ordering their destruction, the viceroy himself arranged for Coatlicue to be taken to the University and advised that these works of antiquity should be studied. And so they were, by Don Antonio de León y Gama. In 1792 de León published his book *Descripción histórica y cronológica de las dos piedras que en ocasión del nuevo empedrado que se está formando en la plaza principal de México se hallaron en ella el año de 1790.* (Historical and chronological description of the two stone works which, on the occasion of the current repaving of the main square of Mexico City, were found there in the year 1790.)

A curious outcome was nonetheless in store. As it turns out, Coatlicue was buried anew, this time in one of the patios at the University. The Dominicans claim that this was to avoid "confronting the youth of Mexico with her," as we are told by Baron Alexander von Humboldt. Upon arriving in Mexico in 1803 and learning of the archeological discoveries, this illustrious traveler wished to study the stone masterpieces and asked to be shown the majestic statue of the goddess. He pleaded with the Bishop of Monterrey, Don Feliciano Marín, to intercede and arrange for the statue to be dug up and shown to him. In the end he was successful.

But what was it that really motivated the stubborn monks in 1803? A letter from Bishop Benito Marín Moxó y Francoly, dated 1805, provides a clue. The letter reads as follows:

The statue was placed . . . in one of the corners of the spacious University patio, where it remained upright for some time, but in the end it was necessary to bury it once again . . . for a reason that none had foreseen. The Indians, who observe all the monuments of European art with such stupid indifference, came with a lively curiosity to contemplate their famous statue. At first it was thought that they were moved to this by no other incentive than national pride, a characteristic of savage no less than of civilized peoples, and by the pleasure of seeing one of the most outstanding works by their ancestors, which they could see was esteemed even by educated Spaniards. Nonetheless, it later came to seem that in their frequent visits there was some secret religious motive. It was thus essential to prohibit their access absolutely; but their fanatical enthusiasm and their incredible cunning made a mockery of this decision.*

They watched for moments when the patio would be empty of people, especially in the afternoon when, at the conclusion of the academic lessons, all the classrooms are closed. Then they would take advantage of the silence that reigns in this home of the Muses, they would leave their towers and hurry to adore their Goddess Teoyaomiqui [Coatlicue]. A thousand times the beadles, returning from outside and crossing the patio on the way to their quarters, caught the Indians by surprise, some on their knees, others prostrate . . . before the statue, and holding in their hands burning candles and other diverse offerings of the sort their elders used to present to their idols. And these things which were done, and later observed with care by many grave and learned persons . . . led to the resolution, as we said, of once more placing the aforesaid statue beneath the ground.

In spite of the Bishop's contempt, his words are highly significant. Let us not forget that this happened only a few years away from the beginnings of the movement for national independence. The tone of the letter reveals how these monuments served to point up the contrast with the mother country. This resurgence of interest in the prehispanic past was significant, as evidenced by everything we have seen up to this point, and we should now add what became of the Sun Stone, which suffered a very different fate.

The enormous sculpture known as the Aztec Calendar was housed in a side chamber of the cathedral —in the west tower— where it remained for many years. This encounter between the Aztec monument and the greatest of the Christian temples is provocative. One must not ignore the role played by these ruins of the past in the critical moments that led to the struggle against the Spanish Crown.

Many years were to pass, nevertheless, before the presence of the past in the center of the city was restored. In the year 1900, on the Calle de las Escalerillas —now Calle Guatemala—Don Leopoldo Batres rescued a piece of the past. During the installation of the drainage works that cross behind the cathedral from east to west, Batres recovered a large quantity of archeological materials. In 1913, Don Manuel Gamio performed excavations on the property located at the corner of the Calles Seminario and Santa Teresa (now Guatemala), and he concluded that the remains found there belonged to the Templo Mayor of Tenochtitlan. Don Manuel was right. While there had been doubts up to that time concerning the location of the great *Teocalli* (Temple), Don Manuel's findings allowed him to present this hypothesis.

The ruins thus uncovered were displayed for many years in view of those who passed that historical corner. And then came the dawn of February 21, 1978. Workers of the Compañía de Luz y Fuerza del Centro (Central Light and Power Company) were laying some cable when they struck a hard object. They stopped work in order to inspect the object that impeded their progress. They removed the mud and were able to see that it was a stone with relief carving. They temporarily suspended their work, and the next day they received a call from the Oficina de Rescate Arqueológico (Office of Archeological Salvage). It was a woman who did not wish to identify herself, but she insisted that a great discovery had taken place at the site. Hours later she called again. The ar-

cheologists came to the corner of Seminario and Guatemala, but were unable to find anything. It was not until the night of February 23 that they were able to corroborate the discovery firsthand.

From that moment on, things happened quickly. The power company's work was suspended indefinitely in order to make way for the archeologists. One week after the initial discovery, the sculpture could be appreciated in all its grandeur. It was Coyolxauhqui, she with the bells painted on her cheeks. She is the sister of Huitzilopochtli, who is the god of sun and war, against whom she fought on the mountain of Coatepec. Coyolxauhqui is the daughter of Coatlicue—she who had re-emerged on August 13, 1790. Now, almost two hundred years later, the daughter came forth to make herself known.

And so the Templo Mayor of the Mexicas began its resurrection.

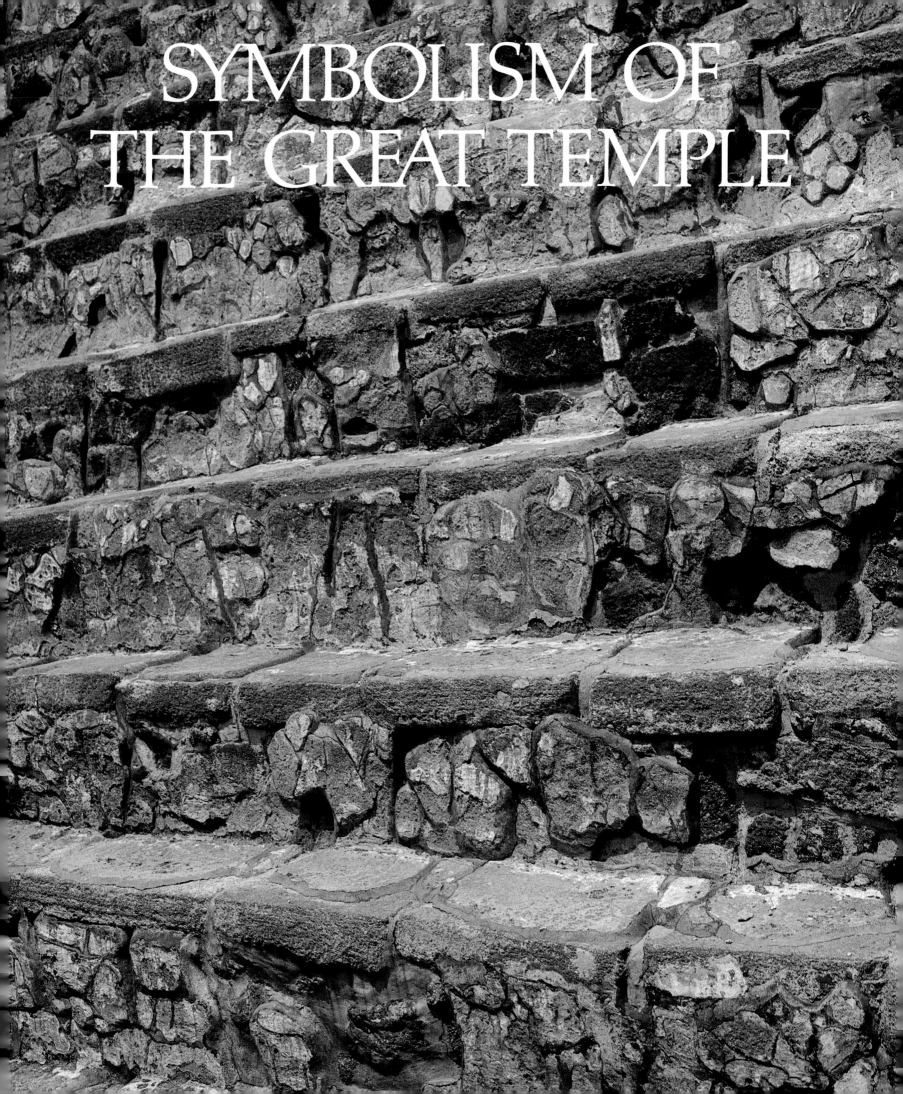

SYMBOLISM OF
THE GREAT TEMPLE

It was difficult to restore the Templo Mayor in an urban environment. It took five years of intensive work, with thousands of eyes watching everything that happened day by day. The concrete foundation of the present city rests on everything that was built up or deposited there several centuries ago: walls, offerings, great serpents' heads and so forth. Nevertheless success was possible. The great time machine of archeology allowed us to penetrate through the concrete and the earth itself to make contact with the faces of yesteryear. To give life to dead objects is the labor of the archeologist. It is not only a matter of finding stone masks and obsidian knives. It is the possibility of going beyond, of discovering what meaning is hidden behind the ruins and penetrating their symbolism. The archeologist who succeeds in this recovers time that has flown, time past.

Taken as a whole, the Templo Mayor is a setting where myths come to life through the contrivance of ritual. Here the face of life and death is ever present. Here are Tlaloc and Huitzilopochtli, present at each sanctuary as an expression of the fundamental needs of the Mexicas. Upon these gods depended the dualities of daily subsistence: water and warfare, agricultural production and imperial tribute, hymn to life and hymn to death: it is this eternal duality of the prehispanic world that here takes on living reality.

That is why the Templo Mayor was for the Mexica the center of the universe. In its very architecture are catalogued the Aztec theories of cosmogenesis. Thus the main platform from which the Templo Mayor rises is the earthly level. At its outer points are found the great, undulating serpents that converge like guardians upon the center. Also on this platform are the serpents' heads at the sides of the two great stairways. At the foot of the stairway on Huitzilopochtli's side was Coyolxauhqui, in the position assigned to her by the myth of the battle of Coatepec. Under this main platform a great many offerings were found. On it we see —to the north and south and at the rear— large braziers in honor of the gods who preside over the temple.

Azcatitla Codex

It is on this platform that the temple itself is built, its four levels rising one on top of the other, with two stairways on the main facade looking to the west. These are the celestial levels leading to the thirteenth heaven, *Omeyocan*, where duality resides. *Omeyocan* is represented by the two sanctuaries dedicated to Tlaloc and Huitzilopochtli.

Each of the two sanctuaries that make up the Templo Mayor represents a myth. Thus, the side dedicated to the god of war symbolizes the mountain of Coatepec, where the fratricidal combat between Huitzilopochtli and Coyolxauhqui took place. Here Huitzilopochtli was born to fight his enemies, which led the Mexicas to believe in their destiny as a warrior people, the people of the sun, since Huitzilopochtli is the sun. Here, to keep the myth alive, the story was represented anew each year in the festival of *Panquetzaliztli*. In this pageant the nocturnal powers represented by Coyolxauhqui and her numberless host of brothers, interpreted as the moon and stars, are conquered day after day by the sun Huitzilopochtli with his weapon *Xiuhcóatl*, the serpent of fire, which is none other than the sun's light as it rises in the east every morning and disperses and outshines the stars.

Tlaloc's side of the temple represents *Tonacatépetl*, or the mountain storehouse of grains, the nourishment of man. Here also a myth is depicted, a myth that speaks to us of how the *tlaloques*, the rain god's helpers, jealously guard the kernels of corn. It was here that Quetzalcóatl came to retrieve the grain and deliver it to men. This is the side of fertility, of life, of the needs of an agricultural people who required water and land in order to survive. Here also is where certain ceremonies took place to appease Tlaloc, for this god also had his negative side: he could scourge the land and kill the crops with hail, lightning and floods.

In these two presences, these two gods, we see the close relationship between life and death. Between the two ''mountains'' that comprise the Templo Mayor, one could as easily pass to the heavens as to the underworld. One of the first steps on the way to *Mictlan*, the land of the dead, was to cross two mountains that knock against one another. The dead are appointed to go to three different places, depending on the type of death they suffer. Those who die in relation to the water god —that is, the victims of drowning, dropsy, etc.— go to *Tlalocan*, the paradise of Tlaloc. Warriors sacrificed or felled in combat go to accompany the sun —Huitzilopochtli— on part of his rounds. Those who die a natural death are destined for *Mictlan*, abode of the skeletons. All this is shown in the images of the Templo Mayor.

Home of the principal myths, the Templo Mayor was the most holy of holies. It was the center of the universe, the great cosmogonic navel harboring an entire symbology of life and death. Let us now see what was hidden and jealously guarded in the bowels of the Templo Mayor of Tenochtitlan. Having broken through the concrete, let us pierce time as well in order to give life to what once was here.

The ancient gods have come back to life.

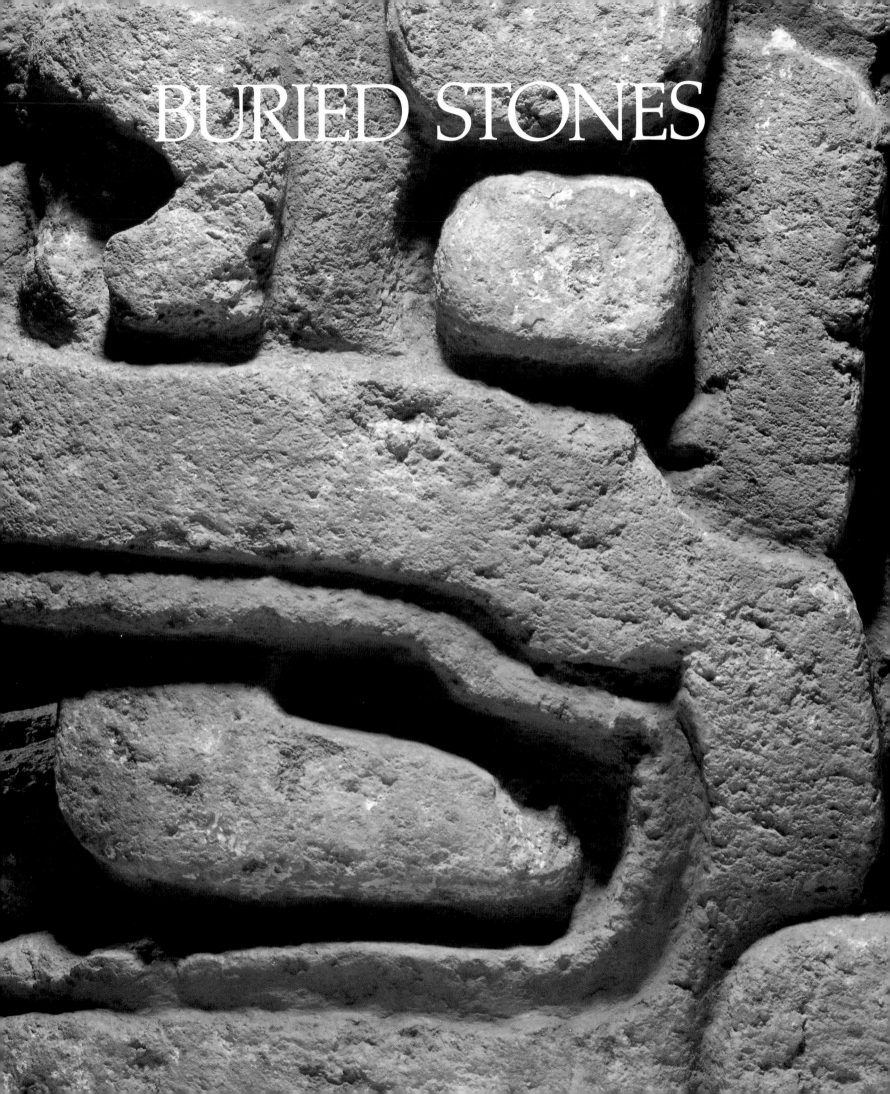

BURIED STONES

Let us imagine ourselves at the most historical corner in Mexico City. There, to one side of the Metropolitan Cathedral, in what used to be the corner of the Calles de Relox (now Argentina), Santa Teresa, Escalerillas (now Guatemala) and Seminario (which still has its old name, although it is no longer open to traffic as it is now part of the Plaza Manuel Gamio) are the ruins of the Templo Mayor. What for many years remained a mystery —that is, the exact location of the principal Mexica temple, for there were those who erroneously believed it to lie beneath the cathedral itself— was unveiled by Gamio's digs at the turn of the century. The ancient location finally was confirmed beyond doubt with the recent Templo Mayor excavation. In the nineteenth century there were already those, like Don Alfredo Chavero, who had decided that the Templo Mayor must be located at the crossing of Iztapalapa, Tacuba and Tepeyac, the ancient causeways that joined Tenochtitlan to dry land. And they were right.

The first thing that strikes the viewer as he stands before the mutilated remains of the Templo Mayor is the perception that they emerge from below the ground and rise above the current street level. In fact, despite the destruction wrought by the Spaniards, the temple mound remained intact. Those who have walked these streets will remember that the Calle Guatemala was somewhat elevated, due in fact to the archeological remains lying under it. Nevertheless, one must descend in order to reach the tiled floors of the ceremonial platform on which the architectural remains of the temple were found to rest.

The Templo Mayor is not one temple but many. Over time, various temples were superimposed one on the other, partly according to the dictates of unstable ground and constant flooding. More importantly, when a new *Tlatoani* came to power and wanted to ingratiate himself with the people and the gods, he usually ordered an enlargement of the Templo Mayor. Thus, like an enormous onion gradually enclosing its center with more and more layers, the temple grew in size, with the previous temple always serving as nucleus and base of the new one. Moreover, each new construction completely buried the old, leaving all of the various sculptures and offerings of the previous layers entombed. On at least seven occasions a new temple was built, always on top of the preceding one. In addition, there were partial expansions, especially of the main facade.

Let us take a tour of these many remodelings and expansions in order to get to know this place where so many artifacts were found, artifacts that speak of the past of a people who came to control a large part of Mesoamerica.

Aerial view of the archeological site with Metropolitan cathedral in background.

Historians such as Durán and Tezozomoc tell us that upon arriving in the middle of Lake Texcoco, the Mexicas saw the sign their god Huitzilopochtli had promised: an eagle perched on a prickly pear cactus. Clearly this important myth was created after the fact, for we know that when the Aztecs arrived in the valley they occupied lands that belonged to others. They were allowed to settle in these regions provided that they rendered tribute. That is to say, the Aztecs settled not where they wanted to, but where the local overlords granted them space. They came to populate the islets where they built Tenochtitlan because that is where the Lord of Azcapotzalco agreed to tolerate them.

One of the first projects they undertook soon after their arrival was to consolidate the terrain and divide the city into four precincts meeting at the center, where they began construction of the Templo Mayor (Phase I). The material they used was locally gathered wood and stone, so that the first temple must have been a relatively low structure. Nothing has been found of this temple; it must be situated at a greater depth than we have reached with our current excavation. On the other hand, a structure now known as Phase II has been located which has been provisional-

ly dated to the year 1390 A.D. Luckily it is almost intact, and the upper sanctuaries of this phase are now exposed.

Huitzilipochtli's sanctuary is characterized by the fact that opposite its entrance is found the sacrificial stone made of *tezontle*, a volcanic stone readily available in the Valley of Mexico. Toward the rear are found the remains of the sanctuary's interior. Here we see a bench that runs north to south. In the middle of this bench is a small altar where the figure of the god must surely have stood. On the uppermost step leading to the sanctuary, in line with the sacrificial stone, we see the face of a figure looking westward from the top of the temple. I venture to suggest that this might represent a figure mentioned in the myth of the battle between Coyolxauhqui and Huitzilopochtli, whose mission was to inform the latter as to the whereabouts of the "Southerners" (Coyolxauhqui's brothers) who were coming to kill Coatlicue. Above his face is a date —2 Rabbit— which, if our interpretation is correct, corresponds to the aforementioned year of 1390 A.D.

The sanctuary on Tlaloc's side of the temple also presents some significant elements. First to come to our atten-

Mendocino Codex

tion is the sculpture of Chac-mool, situated opposite the sanctuary entrance like the sacrificial stone located in front of Huitzilopochtli. The Chac-mool is polychrome and one can still see its colors—blue, red, yellow and white. The role played by this figure is significant: he acts as intermediary between the priest who brings the offering and the god who receives it. He is a sort of divine messenger who takes the offering into the sanctuary's interior. Within the sanctuary, we see again the bench where stood the effigy of the god, in this case the god of water.

Let us not overlook the pillars which form the entryway to the interior of the sanctuary, as they still preserve the polychrome murals that originally covered them. On the outside we see designs in the form of circles that represented the eyes of the god Tlaloc. Underneath these circles are bands of red and blue indicating the celestial level. From them fall vertical bands in black and white which seem to represent rain. Toward the rear, the pillars show a standing yellow figure walking over something which appears to be a current of water painted in blue, black and red.

Most of the remaining parts of this temple (Phase II) have not been uncovered due to the water table, which prevented further excavation. Nevertheless, underneath the floor of these two sanctuaries were found various funerary urns and objects, the most ancient of those uncovered at the Templo Mayor. These will be described in greater detail in later chapters.

Chac-Mool; Polychromed basalt sculpture covered with stucco. Mexica culture.

Mural, Tlaloc's complex; *Polychromed stucco. Mexica culture.*

Mural with yellow figure, Tlaloc's complex; Polychromed stucco. Mexica culture.

The next building phase (Phase III) corresponds to the year 1431, when the Mexicas had recently freed themselves from domination by Azcapotzalco. This period marks the beginning of the expansion of the Mexicas under the reign of Itzcóatl (1427-1440), when the Triple Alliance was formed among Tenochtitlan, Tacuba and Texcoco. The outstanding monuments of this phase are eight sculptures leaning against the stairway on the war god's side of the temple, and three additional sculptures that were found on the stairway to Tlaloc's sanctuary.

Next came Phase IV (ca. 1454 A.D.), during the reign of Montezuma I. This was a time of great expansion, as shown by the grandeur of the new building. To this period belong the ensembles comprised of two braziers, between which stands

Standard-bearers; *Anthropomorphic stone sculptures. Mexica culture.*

a serpent's head resting on the main platform. One of these ensembles adorns the north half of the temple facade, and the other the south half. The same grouping can be found in the rear part of the temple, toward the middle of each of the buildings dedicated to Tlaloc and Huitzilopochtli. The ensemble that corresponds to the god of water has Tlaloc's face on the front part of the brazier, with the attributes that characterize him, such as eye-rings and a forked tongue, all in the original colors of blue, red, yellow, etc. By contrast, the figures on Huitzilopochtli's side wear their hair in a bun, which has been identified as the symbol of the god of war. In the rear of the temple, on the war god's side, a block of stone was found with the numeral 1 Rabbit, which appears to correspond to the year 1454 A.D.

Serpent between two braziers; Basalt. Mexica culture.

During Phase IV various enlargements to the temple were carried out, but only to the main facade of the temple. This took place around 1469 A.D., the same year in which Axayácatl (1469-1485) began his rule. It was in Expansion IV-B where the enormous sculpture of Coyolxauhqui was found on the platform on Huitzilopochtli's side, at the foot of

Rattlesnake's head; Basalt. Mexica culture.

the stairway that leads to the god's sanctuary at the top of the temple. The stairway —like Tlaloc's— has serpents' heads at either end that still retain vestiges of color. The heads on each side of the temple belong to different species. Tlaloc's serpents appear to be rattlesnakes, while the other two have four nostrils, perhaps because they represent a *nauyaca*.

Nauyaca snake's head; *Basalt. Mexica culture.*

Here, on this platform, the altar of the frogs is associated with the god Tlaloc, which is not surprising since these are aquatic creatures.

Frog from Tlaloc's altar; Mexica culture.

Also, on either end of the platform, there are two serpents whose undulating bodies measure more than six meters in length; They face north and south respectively. Exactly in the middle of the platform is another serpent's head colored predominantly red and yellow.

The presence of all these serpents confirms the notion that this side of the Templo Mayor is the mountain of Coatepec (Serpent Mountain), site of the battle between the god of sun and war and his sister Coyolxauhqui, who lies dead at the foot of the temple-mountain.

Head of undulating serpent, (side view and detail); Polychromed basalt. Mexica culture.

51

Bench, Hall of the Eagle Warriors; *Polychromed basalt. Mexica culture.*

Of Phase V (ca. 1485 A.D.), only part of the platform has been preserved, but one finding from this period is of surpassing interest—the Hall of the Eagle Warriors. This area was found in the patio of the great ceremonial hall located on the north side of the Templo Mayor. It consisted of a series of rooms furnished with stone benches on which a complete procession of polychrome figures were found. These are very similar to those at the Palacio Quemado (Burned Palace) in Tula, Hidalgo. In each room the figures converged on a small altar that rose above the benches and held a *zacatapalloli*, the name given to the ball of hay that held the maguey thorns used for self-mortification.

Detail of bench with representations of warriors; Polychromed basalt. Mexica culture.

This area was home to two fantastic clay sculptures of the Eagle Lords, as well as a clay skeleton. Also found here were eight large braziers, of which six bore the effigies of weeping Tlalocs. The entire ensemble shows beyond a doubt that these rooms and the area they comprise were used by the military Order of the Eagle, which together with the Jaguar Warriors made up an important part of the Mexica nobility. A companion building was discovered on the south side of the Templo Mayor. Although it could not be excavated, there is no doubt that it corresponded to the Order of the Jaguar.

*Eagle's head, **Hall of the Eagle Warriors**; Polychromed stone. Mexica culture.*

Certain buildings from Phase VI have also been restored, such as the sanctuaries designated A, B and C, which rise out of the great patio, and the floor of tiles which extended around all four sides of the Templo Mayor during this building phase (ca. 1500 A.D.) These three sanctuaries are located on the north patio, between the central temple structure and the Hall of the Eagle Warriors.

Sanctuary A is a building with two stairways: one on the east facade and the other on the west. By way of contrast, Sanctuary B, which is a Tzompantli, or skullrack altar, has a stairway facing west, while the other side is decorated with panels of skulls carved in rock and covered with stucco. There seems to be a close relationship between this building, located exactly to the north of the Templo Mayor, and the cardinal direction which it occupies. Let us recall that this direction corresponds to *Mictlampa*—the Way of the Dead—which is identified with the color black and the flint knife. The skulls found here—there are more than two hundred of them—mimic the placement of those real skulls in the building that so stunned the conquistadors: the *Tzompantli* or Altar of Skulls.

Tzompantli *Altar of Skulls*; *Stone. Mexica culture.*

54

Detail of wall with rings, Red Temple.
Polychromed stucco. Mexica culture.

Sanctuary C is known as the Red Temple. It has a companion structure on the south side of the Templo Mayor. This building is characterized by the predominance of the color red on a sanctuary which also has the singular characteristic that its east-facing facade is composed of a vestibule with a round altar. This vestibule in turn is made up of two walls topped with large red stone rings. Vestiges of painting can still be seen on a large part of this sanctuary. In general, some of the paintings seem to imitate certain aspects of the paintings at Teotihuacan. The old god Huehuetéotl, who was found very near this structure, in the north patio, probably sat on top of this building. His statue rests in a position similar to the placement of the ancient gods found at Teotihuacan.

*Detail of mural, **Red Temple**; Polychromed stucco. Mexica culture.*

The last construction phase of the Templo Mayor is characterized by the fact that the structure was not enlarged on all four sides as in the previous remodelings, but rested on the same platform as its immediate predecessor. Unfortunately, only a few vestiges remain of this phase, on the north side. Only traces marked out on the flagstone floors of the space occupied by this last phase of the building were found.

Having completed our imaginary first turn around the Templo Mayor of Tenochtitlan, we will next visit the artifacts painstakingly salvaged there over a period of five years.

Let us enter the Museum, then, where this voyage to the past will take us to our encounter with the magnificent art of the Templo Mayor.

FULL OF PRIDE IN HERSELF,

UP RISES THE CITY OF MEXICO-TENOCHTITLAN.

HERE NO ONE FEARS DEATH IN COMBAT.

THIS IS OUR GLORY,

THIS IS OUR MANDATE.

OH, GIVER OF LIFE!

KNOW THIS, OH PRINCES,

DO NOT FORGET IT.

WHO SHALL SUCCEED IN LAYING SIEGE TO TENOCHTITLAN?

WHO SHALL SUCCEED IN SHAKING THE FOUNDATIONS OF THE SKY . . .?

BY OUR ARROWS,

BY OUR SHIELDS,

THE CITY EXISTS.

MEXICO-TENOCHTITLAN LIVES ON!

MEXICA SONGS

AND SUCH WERE THE MARVELS WE SAW THAT WE KNEW NOT WHAT

TO SAY,

OR WHETHER TO BELIEVE WHAT WAS BEFORE OUR EYES,

FOR ON THE ONE HAND WERE GREAT CITIES ON THE LAND,

AND ON THE LAKE MANY MORE, AND WE SAW CANOES EVERYWHERE

AND ALONG THE CAUSEWAY WERE MANY BRIDGES AT REGULAR

INTERVALS,

AND BEFORE US STOOD THE GREAT CITY OF MEXICO.

BERNAL DIAZ DEL CASTILLO

MUSEUM OF
THE GREAT TEMPLE

The plan of the museum is based on information discovered by archeologists and on written sources that describe the Templo Mayor. The eight halls have been divided into two sections corresponding in theme to the major divisions of the temple. The south halls are associated with Huitzilopochtli, while the north halls are related to Tlaloc. A gigantic model of the ceremonial complex provides a centerpiece that separates the two sections. The model incorporates new architectural information gathered over the course of a decade that enriches our knowledge of the ceremonial center.

The tour we are about to take through examining these ancient art objects will illuminate not only Aztec forms of expression, but also the expressions of various other tribes and regions subject to Tenochtitlan, whose artifacts came to reside in the Templo Mayor. In this center of the world, this navel of the Mexica universe, there was also room for the art of the conquered enemy who were forced to give the "people of the sun" —as Alfonso Caso called them—their men and their artworks to honor the fearsome Huitzilopochtli. The Templo Mayor, the Mexicas' seat of glory, was also a place of misfortune and death for those who fell under their sway.

Here, inside Huitzilopochtli's sanctuary, another interesting discovery was made of some of the most ancient objects in the Templo Mayor, corresponding to Phase II (1390 A.D.). Not surprisingly, they are mortuary objects—two funerary urns.

The first one is made of alabaster covered with a unique obsidian lid. Inside it were some charred bones, two pieces of green stone and a gold bell. A short distance away another small urn made entirely of obsidian was found. On one side it shows the face of what seems to be a skull or a monkey. Its delicate lid speaks to us of masterful obsidian artisanry, a craft that dates back to ancient times in Mesoamerica. This material is not easy to work with, especially if the crafted object is a delicate one. Such pieces require great experience and skill. As with the first urn, the inside of this one contained the remains of charred bones.

Funerary urn; *Obsidian (13.3 x 6.5 cm). Mexica culture.*

Anthropomorphic mask; Silver (4.9 x 4.5 x 1.9 cm). Mexica culture.

Although the objects found inside them are of course important, the urns acquire their real significance within the context implied by their location. Both urns were found at the foot of Huitzilopochtli's altar, inside the sanctuary. They must have contained the remains of personages in the uppermost social hierarchy to have received burial here. In spite of this fact, there is no great burial offering nor anything remotely resembling one. This reinforces the theory advanced earlier that Phase II of the temple corresponds to a historical period when the Mexicas were subject to Azcapotzalco and that, although the charred remains deposited here must have been those of distinguished persons, the circumstances of the tribe did not permit grand funeral rites.

What was most striking about it at the time of discovery was the fact that two extremely interesting objects were found stuck to the lid: a gold bell it bore on top which seems to be the symbol of *ollín* (movement), and a small silver mask with a very peculiar face. The face gives the impression of having its flesh eaten away, although its nose also ends in a protuberance. Along the top of its head is a filigree ornament, and from its ears hang large earrings in the form of rattlesnakes. In effect, one sees first the snake's rattle and then the body forming a knot that ends in a sophisticated snake's head.

Bell with ollin *(movement) symbol; Gold (2.7 x 2.2 cm). Mexica culture.*

69

Another interesting piece is a small ceramic figure of a dog, also found within the sanctuary of Huitzilopochtli, god of war. This piece was made of a foreign clay known to archeologists as *plumbate*. It was obtained in trade from the area of Guatemala. In general the use of this type of clay was at its peak about 1100 A.D., at the height of Toltec splendor. Symbolically, the dog played an important part in prehispanic Mexico. It was closely related to death, and was an indispensable aid to the type of dead soul known as *Teyolía*, who must cross the rivers that form part of the passage to *Mictlan*, the home of the dead. In this particular sculpture, the outstanding feature is the great realism of the head, which is topped by a kind of crest. The dog's paws support the receptacle formed by its body.

***Zoomorphic funerary urn representing dog**, (front and side views); Plumbate pottery (14.5 x 13 x 18 cm). Toltec culture.*

The discovery of objects from as far away as Guatemala indicates that trade went on between the various Mesoamerican regions from very remote times. It is worth remembering that, during their period of greatest expansion, the Mexicas achieved a vast sphere of influence. They came to control the entire central portion of Mexico, with only the Tlaxcalans remaining free of their dominion. To the south, they controlled the present state of Morelos and an area that is now part of Guerrero. From these outlying areas they obtained fruit, cotton and other important products. Part of the Mixtec area of Oaxaca was also subject to Mexica power, as was much of the Gulf Coast, and the Mexicas were preparing invasions of the Maya regions at the time of the Spaniards' arrival.

On the other hand, one place they were never able to subjugate, a place where they suffered great defeats, was among the Purépechas of Michoacán. A major defeat occurrred during the reign of Axayácatl (1469-1481 A.D.). One of the orange clay funerary urns found very near the statue of Coyolxauhqui may have contained the cremated remains of Aztec captains felled in these battles.

Both urns are of exceptional quality and they are related to one another, as evidenced by the gods pictured on them. On the first urn is the figure of Tezcatlipoca, armed with an *átlatl* —or dart sling— in his left hand, while in his right he holds two darts. A salient feature is the god's foot, for in its place is the smoking mirror that symbolizes Tezcatlipoca. The background to the relief is formed by a serpent bearing a beautiful, elaborate headdress. The upper edge of the urn is decorated with what might be called stylized snails. Inside the urn, in addition to charred bones, was found a necklace made of little obsidian ducks' heads.

The second urn represents a god who has not been definitively identified. Like Tezcatlipoca, he bears a sling

Funerary urn with figure of Tezcatlipoca in high relief; Orange pottery (34.1 x 17.5 cm). Gulf culture.

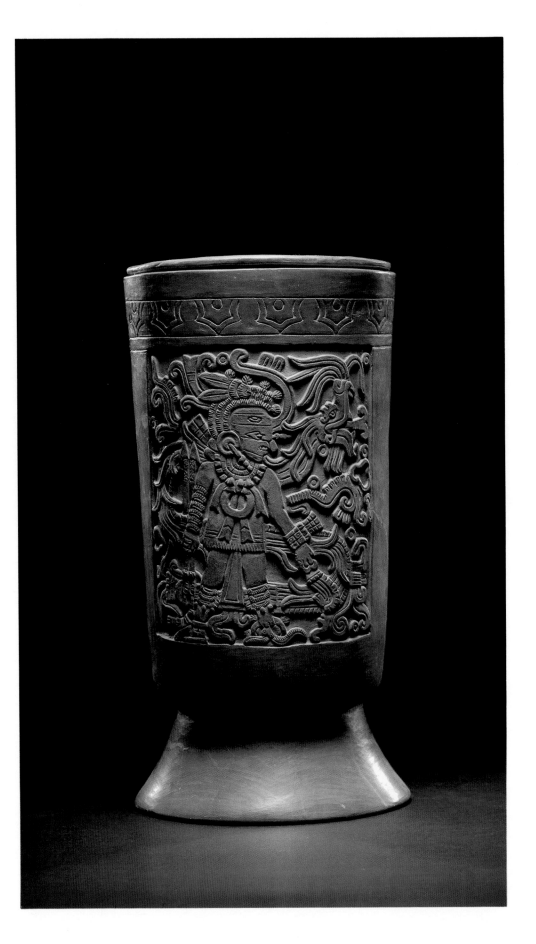

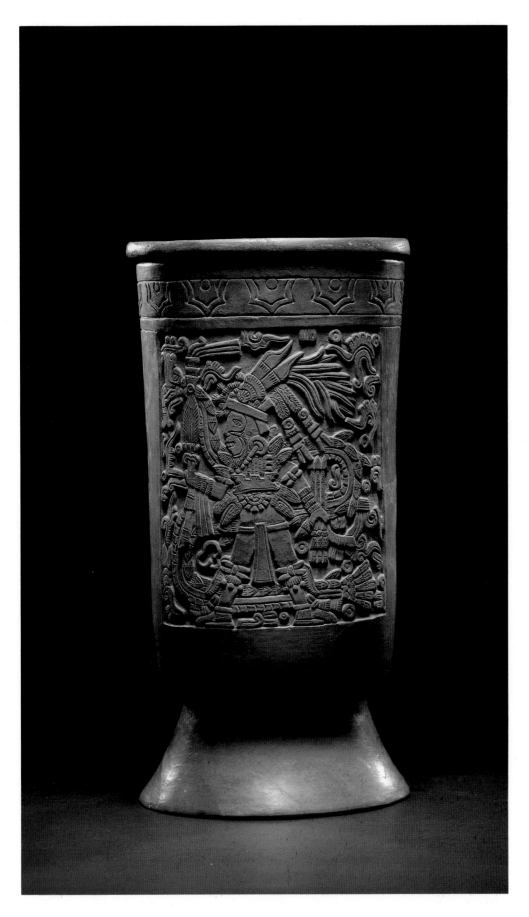

in his right hand and darts in the other. On his chest is a breastplate that recalls those worn by the fire god Xiuhtecuhtli. The god is bearded and wears a headdress of long feathers with two prominent elements whose signifiance is still unknown. Here again the background is formed by a serpent, although the designs on the serpent's back are different from those on the other urn. Inside the urn was a sort of breastplate in the form of a serpent, with a visible rattle and head. Both urns were topped by clay lids.

The style of these two pieces would seem to indicate that they came from the center of Veracruz, where similar objects have been found. What is significant is the setting in which they were found: underneath the floor of the Phase IV-B platform (ca. 1470 A.D.) and very near the statue of Coyolxauhqui—that is, on the war god's side of the temple. That the figures represent armed gods and probably correspond in time to the reign of Axayácatl leads to the conclusion suggested earlier: that these may be two distinguished captains who found death in what was for the Mexicas the most unfortunate of wars, their clash with the Purépechas.

Funerary urn with unidentified figure in high relief; Orange pottery (33.2 x 17.4 cm). Gulf culture.

In the same exhibit with the preceding funerary urns is a stone cup whose death motif is obvious. On one side it has a figure of a standing skeleton with its hands upraised. It is dressed in a small skirt with a loincloth that hangs down in the front. It is also wearing a necklace and earrings, and its headdress is typical of the gods of the underworld. Interestingly, its feet and hands have skin, while its face is totally denuded of flesh. This is not unusual; most of the numerous cup-figures in which human bones have been found are semi-emaciated, as are the *cihuateteos*, or women who died in childbirth, on display at the Museo Nacional de Antropología. Their faces are skulls, while their breasts and hands, in the form of claws, still wear their flesh. There are many other similar examples.

On the stone cup, the figure represented by the semi-skeleton is that of the god Mictlantecuhtli, lord of *Mictlan*, land of the dead. Despite the difficulty of sculpting this very hard stone, the artist was supremely successful in giving us a work full of the sense of death.

*Ceremonial cup with figure of **Mictlantecuhtli**, (front and side views); Green stone (16.7 x 12 x 8.7 cm). Mexica culture.*

Of the many elements of death and sacrifice that the Mexicas have left us in the Templo Mayor, some of the most significant are the mortuary masks made of stone and placed over the remains of the dead. The masks were used as sculptures to represent certain gods, and also as masks in certain rites. Diverse offerings yielded masks from different regions, the most numerous being from the area of Mezcala, in the present state of Guerrero. Some interesting studies have been made of such masks.

Nonetheless, of all the Mexica masks that have been found, none is more interesting than the alabaster mask shown here. It is typical in most of its characteristics, yet the whiteness of the stone makes it an unusual specimen. When it was discovered, it still bore the shell and pyrite encrustations that formed the red eyes that give it such a singular expression. The teeth, also made of shell, were not found intact, but a few of them remain. There are very few of these alabaster masks, which makes this one a rare and magnificent specimen of this type of stonework. The raw material for this work came from the region of the present state of Puebla, from which it was no doubt brought to Tenochtitlan as tribute.

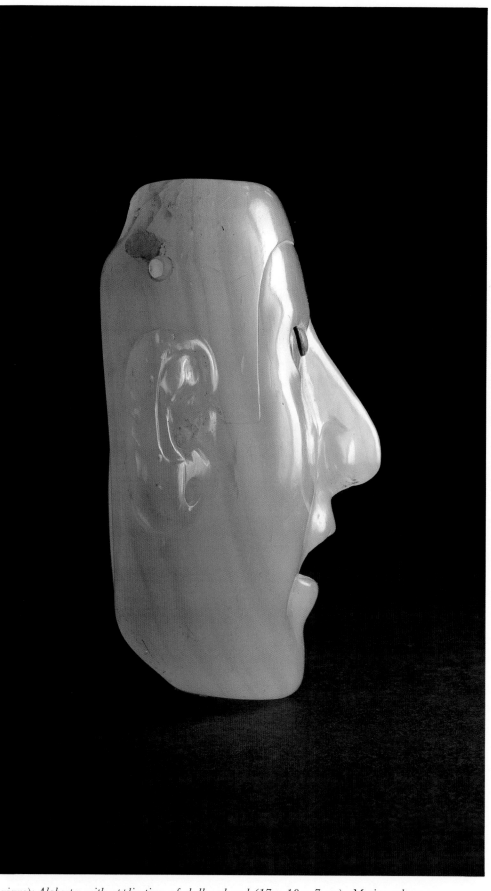

Anthropomorphic mask of **tecalli**, *(side and front views); Alabaster with applications of shell and seed (17 x 18 x 7 cm). Mexica culture.*

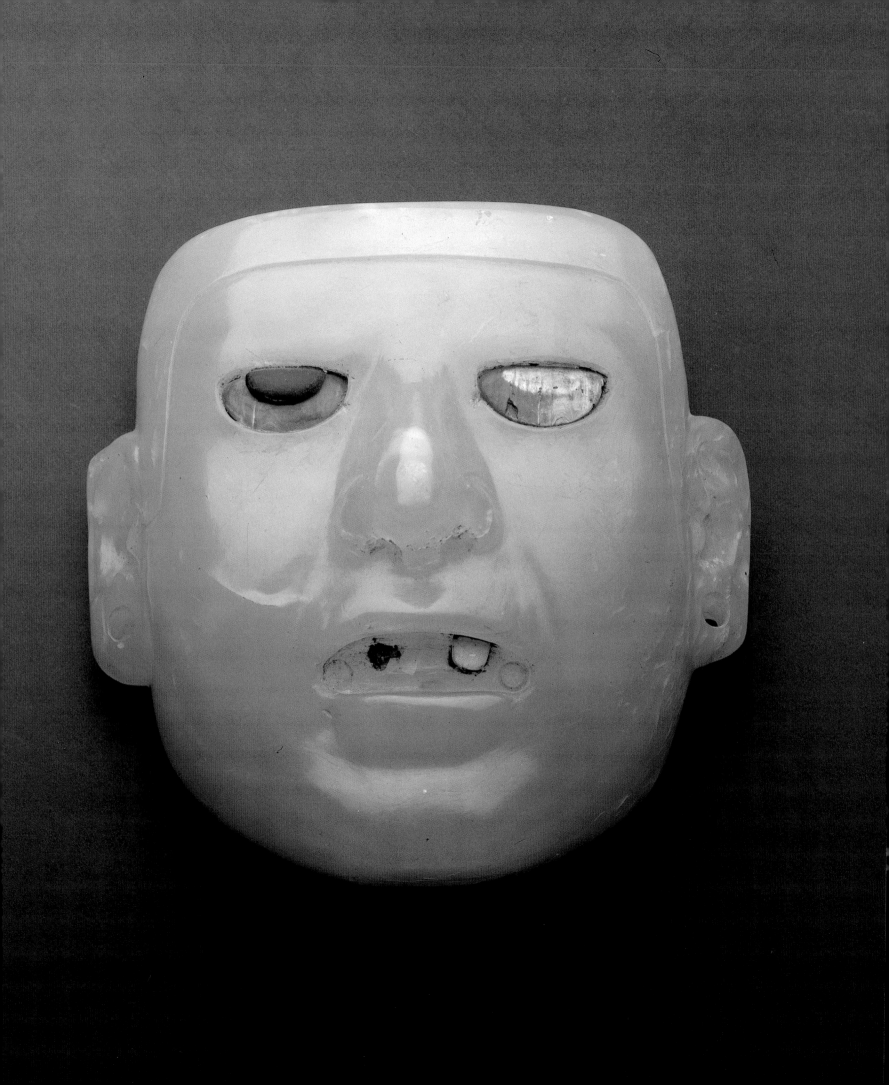

Of all of these expressions of death, the most outstanding are those that use the human skull and transform it into the ultimate image of death. Such is the character of the *Tzompantlis*, the places of skulls. Descriptions of these occur in various chronicles, and we know from archeological evidence that they were elongated platforms of wooden posts and crosspieces on which the skulls were strung.

The perforated skulls that no doubt hung on the *Tzompantli* have been found. These skulls served as a kind of war trophy, and they must have made a profound impression on the enemy. There are other symbolic expressions of death likewise made out of skulls—skulls that have been carefully cut behind the brow line so as to leave the facial portion for use as a mask. These skull-masks truly have a horrible beauty. The grisly life imparted by their shell and pyrite eyes succeeds in giving them a particularly terrifying aspect. Sometimes a silex knife is thrust into the nasal cavity and shells are placed along the mouth. The effect thus achieved is utterly horrifying.

We do not know exactly how skulls thus prepared were used. They are generally pierced along the brow with small holes that may have served to hold some type of decoration, such as feathers or paper—although there is some speculation that they were designed to allow the user to hang them over his face as a sort of mask. The knife in the nose may signify death in the cutting off of the flow of life-giving air.

Tecpatl *knife; Silex, copal base, shells, Mexica culture.*

Skull mask; *Bone, applications of shell and pyrite, with silex knife (18.5 x 13.5 cm). Mexica culture.*

There are knives like these in the mouths of certain gods, as in the case of certain *tlaltecuhtlis*, or earth monsters—figures of the deity whose purpose was to devour human corpses and eat the blood and skin, leaving them bare of all flesh. In some prayers to Tezcatlipoca, we have a picture of this divine action. Here is Sahagún's rendition of one such prayer:

The earth god opens his mouth hungrily to devour the blood of many who will die in this war.

The sun and the earth god called Tlaltecuhtli seem to rejoice; they wish to give food and drink to the gods of heaven and hell, inviting them to partake of the flesh and blood of the men who are to die in this war . . .

May it please you, oh Lord! that the nobles who die in combat be peacefully and joyfully received by the Sun and the Earth, who are the father and mother of all, whose bowels are of love.

For in truth you do not deceive yourselves in what you do, that is, in wanting them to die in battle, for truly it was for this that you sent them to this earth, that they might feed the sun and the earth with their flesh and blood.

There are various figures of Tlaltecuhtli from the Templo Mayor. They are shown with long fangs and claw-like hands that hold small skulls. Skulls also appear as decorations on the god's legs. This was a god who had to appear facedown, next to the earth, and who generally was invisible (as we mentioned earlier). A figure of Tlaltecuhtli appears underneath the statue of Coatlicue discovered in 1790.

Tablet representing the god Tlaltecuhtli;
Basalt (72 x 61 x 24.7 cm). Mexica culture.

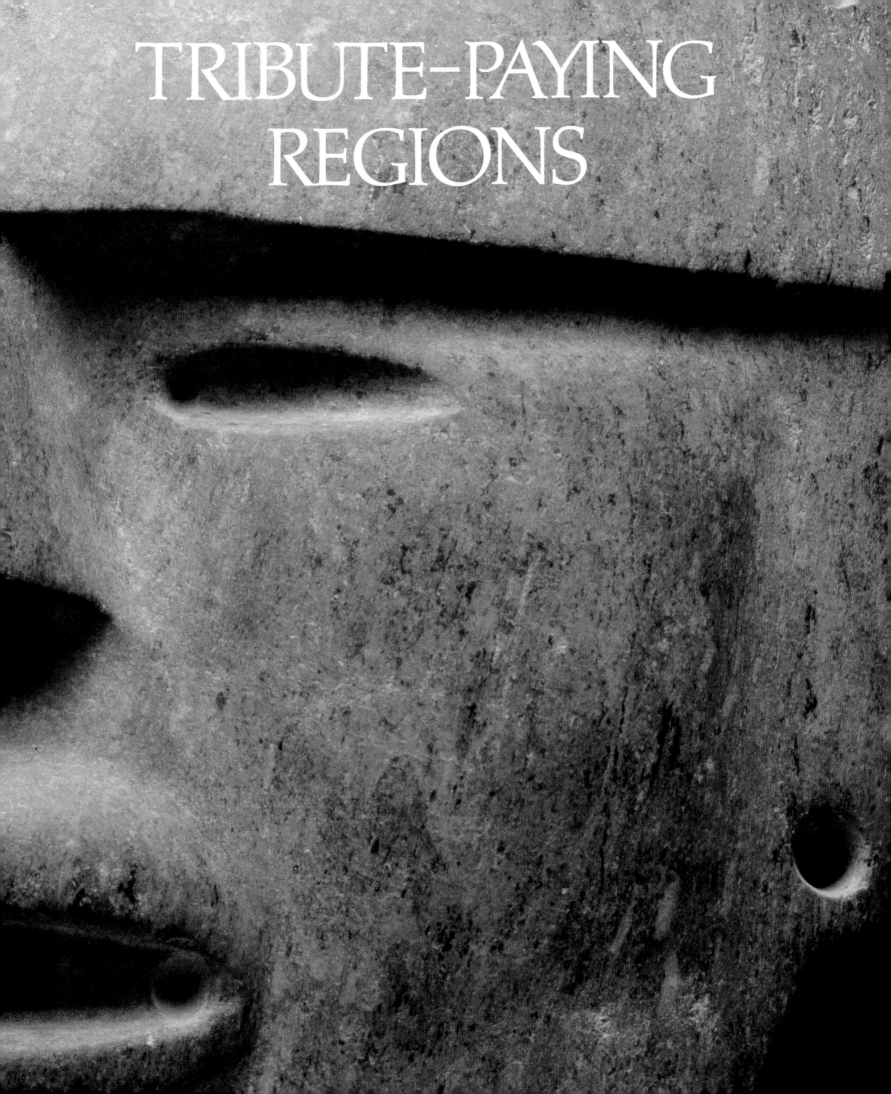

TRIBUTE-PAYING
REGIONS

The many artifacts from the tribute-paying regions found in the Templo Mayor indicate the extent and power of Huitzilopochtli's cult. We have already described funerary urns from the Gulf Coast and an alabaster mask. We now look at other objects, not only because they indicate the extent of the Mexicas' control over other areas, but also in order to appreciate the artistic expression of the peoples subject to Tenochtitlan's rule.

One of these tribute-paying areas is now part of the state of Hidalgo. It provided the Mexicas, among other things, with obsidian, a very common volcanic stone. It served in the manufacture of a diversity of objects from dart points, arrows and lances used in warfare to art pieces whose refinement and finished perfection are astonishing.

Among these are several artifacts worth noting. For example, an enormous mace capped by a knob, which seems to be made in two segments; or miniature maces that served as pestles, together with minute plates made of the same material, possibly used for grinding pigments; or the serpents' heads and the snake's rattle that evince such astonishing realism. In short, these pieces demonstrate the creative power of sculptors who obviously achieved the highest levels of perfection and beauty of form.

Mace and other artifacts; Obsidian. Mexica culture.

Snake's heads; Obsidian; Mexica culture.

Another important area represented in the Templo Mayor is the Mixteca. Here originated many sculptures of *penates* (household gods) notable for certain unique characteristics. These are blocks of light green, almost white stone from quarries apparently located in Oaxaca or Guerrero.

In general, these household deities are about twelve centimeters tall, with various slashes designed to indicate arms, legs and other shapes.

Their miniature faces are quite detailed. In most cases they are identified with the face of Tlaloc, the rain god, as they have the typical eye-rings and the distinctive mustache that characterize him. In addition, they show vertical grooves that give the impression of teeth. There is one figure that seems to be a wind god, if only because he is wearing a sort of mouth-mask which is known to be an attribute of Wind. These sculptures were found with a variety of offerings on both Huitzilopochtli's and

Tlaloc's side of the temple. The fact that they represent the latter deity is significant. The need of agricultural societies such as this one for water was basic.

A product of the tribute system, these figures also demonstrate the Mexica's control over the economic and political areas under their rule. The expansion into what is now Oaxaca began during the reign of Montezuma I.

***Group of* penates**, *(detail on following page); Various stones. Mixtec culture.*

Gold also came from the area of Oaxaca. It is now known that the Mixtecs worked this metal from very ancient times in Mesoamerica, and they achieved outstanding skill in goldsmithing. The pieces found by Don Alfonso Caso in Tomb VII at Monte Albán stand in testimony of this. At the Templo Mayor, various gold objects were found. Some were simple round sheets with a central hole, and may have served as decorative objects for headdresses or articles of clothing, while others were necklace beads, bracelets and earrings of splendid craftsmanship. Although rare, this ''excrement of the gods,'' as it was thought of in the prehispanic world, could hardly fail to make its presence felt in a setting where gods and myths came into full being only in relation to that mission which the Mexica felt was his own: conquest through warfare.

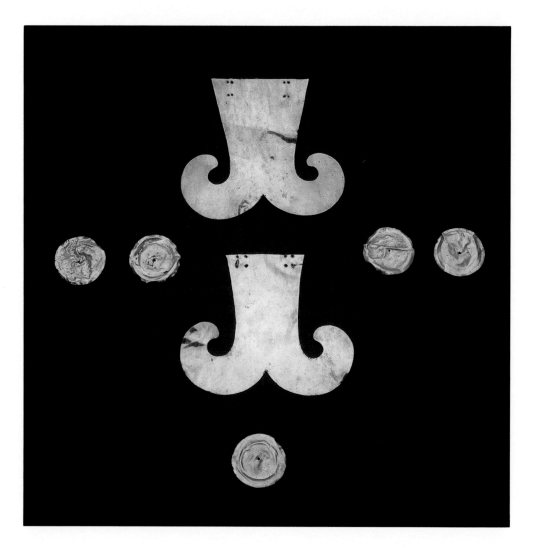

Ornaments; Gold (6.3 x 6.6 cm). Mexica culture.

Bead and bell jewelry; Silver; Mexica culture.

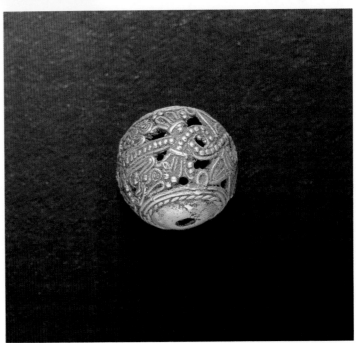

False-filigree bead; Gold, Diameter: 2 cm. Mexica culture.

When we speak of conquered regions, we must naturally mention the importance of Guerrero. This area, located directly to the south of Tenochtitlan, gave rise to many important products, among them the green stone known as *chalchihuite*. Furthermore, this was known as the southern region of the universe and was thus ruled by none other than Huitzilopochtli. This explains the unique significance of the South to the Mexica universe.

Mezcala figure; Stone with red pigment (18 x 7 x 2 cm). Guerrero area culture.

Mezcala-style figure; Green stone with red and white pigment (20 x 8 x 10 cm). Guerrero area culture.

The sun in its annual journey has moved south in the month of December, at the time of the winter solstice. For those among the Mexicas and other Mesoamerican peoples who observed the sky, this displacement of the sun at the height of the dry season did not go unnoticed. Through it the warrior gods showed the Mexicas the proper season to turn south for combat, just as in myth Huitzilopochtli battles the Southerners (the southern stars), whom he conquers and disperses.

Mezcala-style monkey; Green stone (16.5 x 10.5 cm). Guerrero area culture.

Seated figure of hunch-backed man; Green stone (18 x 15 x 6 cm). Guerrero area culture.

Anthropomorphic figure; *Green stone with incrustations of shell and obsidian (29 x 17 x 9 cm). Guerrero area culture.*

Anthropomorphic male figure; *Green stone (23.2 x 5.8 x 9 cm). Guerrero area culture.*

But there is another aspect to all this. This was also the season when the enemy's granaries would be full of the harvest from the previous rainy season, which came to a close in the month of September. In this way the Mexicas politically conquered the areas singled out by the sun god while also replenishing their supplies from the enemy's store of grains. This also happened to be the season when the Mexicas could count on manpower for the battle, as the growing season was over. In addition, this was a cycle of events based with great precision on an ongoing observation of nature and the movement of the stars. The Mexica thus succeeded in justifying his warlike mission theologically, and at the same time filled his larder with foreign goods won by military might.

Mezcala-style female figure; Green stone (31.5 x 19.5 x 3.6 cm). Guerrero area culture.

A diversity of masks and full-body figures, many of them identified as belonging to the Mezcala style, came from this general area that now comprises the state of Guerrero. There were offerings such as those found in Chamber II made up almost entirely of great quantities of masks and figures. Some of the masks are very thin, with barely discernible facial features, giving them a look of extreme simplicity. Others are decorated and still retain vestiges of painting, with more than one of them representing the features of the rain god Tlaloc. A few of them are marked on the back side with black glyphs, perhaps the name of a tribe which thus left a record of having paid the tribute exacted by Tenochtitlan.

Anthropomorphic mask possibly representing the god Tlaloc; Green stone with red and white pigment (16 x 10.5 x 2 cm). Guerrero area culture.

Group of Mezcala-style masks; Green stone. Guerrero area culture.

Although this has not been confirmed, it is interesting to note the variety of glyphs borne by some of these masks. One of the masks is particularly distinguished esthetically. It has two depressions for eyes and the mouth is barely sketched in. The nose is virtually non-existent, but the form is complete without it. A stylized descending bird can be seen on the forehead, along with some vestiges of red, white and black paint.

Mezcala-style anthropomorphic mask; Polychromed stone (20 x 14.4 x 3.8 cm). Guerrero area culture.

Anthropomorphic mask; *Stone with incrustations of shell and obsidian (21.6 x 19 x 3.9 cm). Guerrero area culture.*

There are also various types of full-body figures, several of which still retain their eyes of shell and obsidian. Among them is one of particular note that recalls certain South American, specifically Colombian, artifacts. This one depicts a human figure with his legs spread wide and his hands resting on his knees.

The esthetic character expressed in these masks and figures deserves its own study, for they constitute a series of forms in which the power of expressive simplification reaches remarkable heights.

***Anthropomorphic male figurine**, (side and front views); Green stone with black pigment and incrustations of shell and obsidian (24.5 x 16 x 7.3 cm). Guerrero area culture.*

Also in the warriors' hall stand the stone statues that represent the so-called standard-bearers. Altogether there are eight figures dressed in simple loincloths, some with their hands on their chest and others with the right arm upraised as if holding something. Incrustations, some of which are still present, marked the eyes and mouth. The figures correspond to a an earlier period than the eagle warriors. They probably date to just after the Mexicas' liberation from Azcapotzalco, as they were found in Phase III, which has been fixed chronologically at about 1431 A.D., during the reign of Itzcoatl. They may represent the *Huitznahua*, brothers of Huitzilopochtli, who fought against him on Coatepec mountain. This myth will be discussed later.

Standard-Bearer; *Stone sculpture with incrustations of shell and obsidian (202 x 47.6 x 27.5 cm) Mexica culture.*
(Side view shows figures as they were discovered at site).

One stone figure is very striking: the figure of the old fire-god, Huehue-téotl, known to the Mexicas as Xiuh-tecuhtli. He is shown in the same posture he held in Teotihuacan thousands of years earlier—seated, with his hands on his knees. His right hand is open, while the left forms a fist. He is wearing a large necklace with a pectoral pendant, and massive round earrings frame his strange face. His eyes are covered with a sort of mask and his mouth wears a plate with large fangs on either side. He is hunched over and wears on his head an enormous brazier that is dec-orated all around with various de-signs.

On the figure's back can be seen its hair ornament and a numeral. The brazier bears a significant scene. One can see streams of water and whirl-pools with two snails above them. Overall the figure shows great plas-ticity. Seen from the front, the head and brazier together make up more than half of the piece, which beau-tifully conveys the artist's intent of portraying someone who is old and bent. Because it was found on the temple's north patio, very near the Red Temple that recalls the temples of Teotihuacan, there is little doubt that this sculpture of Huehuetéotl was placed over the latter sanctuary, or perhaps on the circular altar that

stands before it. The nature of this god is significant. It was he who rested at the center of the universe and held it in balance. This is expressed by the ancient hymns.

Mother of the gods, father of the gods,
The old god, lying in the navel of the earth,
enclosed in a turquoise chamber.
He who is in the waters that are the color
*   of the blue bird,*
He who is wrapped in clouds,
The old god, He who lives in the shadow of
*   the land of the dead,*
Lord of fire and lord of the year.

Huehueteotl, or Old Fire god, *(rear, side and front views); Stone sculpture (77 x 56 cm). Mexica culture.*

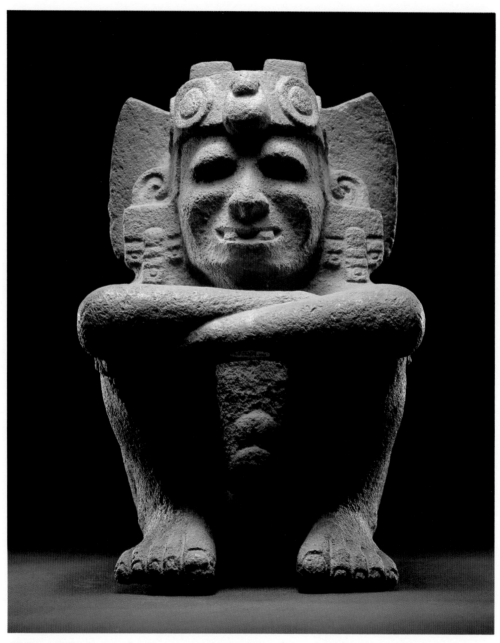

Xiuhtecuhtli, *(front and side views); Basalt with red, blue and black pigment (36 x 56 cm).*
Mexica culture.

While on the subject of the gods, there is a figure of a female deity that must not go unnoticed. This is a block of green stone about 1.4 meters (about 4.5 feet) long which surely comes from the area of Guerrero. According to studies by Alfredo Lopez Austin, it represents Mayahuel, the goddess of *pulque* (a liquor made from fermented maguey). This piece appeared in Chamber I, underneath the great stairway that leads to the temple of Huitzilopochtli. Her association with Coyolxauhqui is thus very close; she was found only a few meters away from the latter. Her statue occupied the center of the chamber and was surrounded by a great quantity of green beads and other objects. The transfer of this massive block of stone from distant regions must have entailed many obstacles, but nothing could stand in the way of portraying Tenochtitlan's might.

Goddess Mayahuel; *Green stone (135 x 41 x 20 cm). Mexica culture.*

During our tour of the south side of the museum, and hence of the Templo Mayor, we have seen everything connected with the enormous imperial expansion achieved by the Mexicas in less than a hundred years. We have seen their power reflected in the presence of materials from the many peoples that paid them tribute—371 tribes, according to scholars. We have seen all the faces of death, of sacrifice, of the world of war. Now let us turn to the actual moment of death. What becomes of an individual killed in combat or sacrificed to the gods?

A point of departure is provided by a clay skeleton now located on the bench running along the Hall of the Eagle Warriors. This skeleton and another like it were found in the interior of the hall, flanking the entry to a small corridor that led into another set of chambers. Unfortunately, the skull was not found, as the floor of a colonial building that passed exactly above the figure destroyed its head. The association between representations of warriors and of skeletons, as exemplified by this find, is highly indicative of Mexica thought.

__God Mictlantecuhtli__; Ceramic (107 x 38 x 43 cm). Mexica culture.

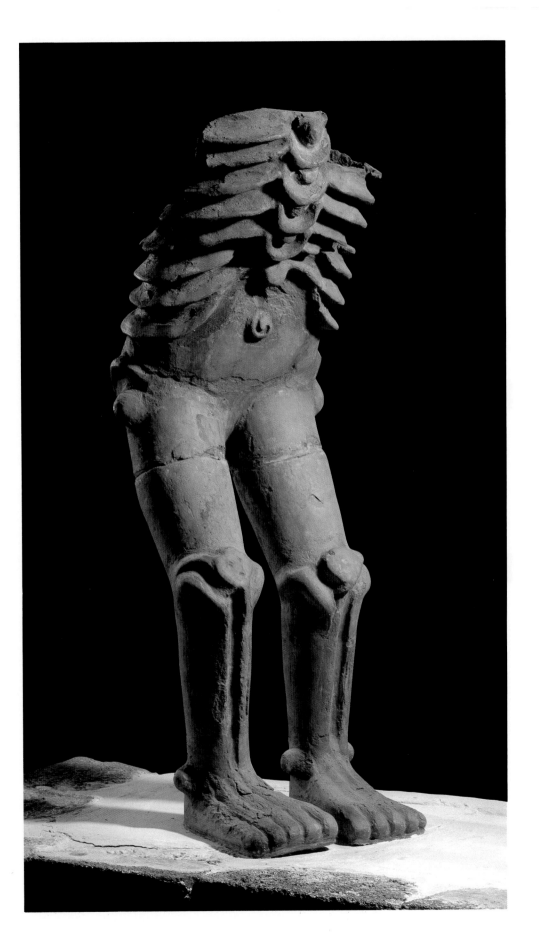

But let us return to the question: what was the ultimate fate of the Mexican individual? We know that the dead went to three different places based on the cause of death. Mictlan, abode of the skeletons, was the home of individuals who died a natural death. Tlalocan, paradise of the god Tlaloc, was the destination of those who died in relation to water, whether by drowning or because of dropsy or some other related cause. The third possible fate of the dead was to accompany the sun. This last fate was reserved exclusively for those who died in combat or by sacrifice, and for women who died in childbirth, as this too was considered a form of battle.

Three figures from the Templo Mayor bring together the three protagonists of this third fate. A figure of a warrior with his locks of hair, his whole body painted blue, sits, apparently waiting for whatever his destiny brings. Upon dying in the appropriate manner, his body must pass through the god Tlaltecuhtli, represented by a figure with enor-

Cihuateotl; Rear view of female figure, basalt (82.5 x 53 x 50 cm). Mexica culture.

120

mous fangs and skull ornaments that echo his mission as the great devourer of corpses. The trilogy is rounded out by the figure of a woman who has died in childbirth, a *cihuateteo*, whose death by this means entitles her to accompany the sun in its westward journey, toward the land of *cihuatlampa*, the place of women.

With this final fate, the warrior's ultimate transcendence was assured. At the end of four years he would be transformed into a bird of beautiful plumage. As a nahuatl poem says:

Male figure; Polychromed stucco on stone (92.5 x 40 x 60 cm). Mexica culture.

Emeralds and
Turquoise
Are your clay and your plumage,
Oh thou for whom all lives!

Now the princes
Are content
With flowering death on the knife edge
    of obsidian,
With death in combat . . .

LEGEND OF COYOLXAUHQUI

Greatly did the Mexicas honor Huitzilopochtli,
They knew that his origin, his beginning
Was thus:

In Coatepec, in the direction of Tula,
There was a woman,
A woman had been living there
Whose name was Coatlicue.

She was the mother of the four hundred Southerners
And of their sister
Whose name was Coyolxauhqui.

And this Coatlicue was doing penance,
She swept, it was her duty to sweep,
This was how she did penance on Coatepec,
  The Serpent's Mountain.

And once,
As Coatlicue was sweeping,
There descended upon her a plumage
Like a ball of fine, soft feathers.

At once Coatlicue gathered it up;
She placed it in her bosom.

When she had done sweeping,
She sought the feather, which she had placed
In her bosom,
But she saw nothing there.

At that very moment Coatlicue became pregnant.

When the four hundred Southerners
Saw that their mother was pregnant,
Many of them grew angry. They said:

"Who has done this thing?
Who has got her with child?
He insults us, he dishonors us."

And their sister Coyolxauhqui said to them:

"Brothers, she has dishonored us.
We must kill our mother,
This perverse woman who is pregnant now.
Who has begot this thing she bears in her bosom?"

When Coatlicue heard of this,
She was sorely frightened,
She was sorely distressed.
But her son Huitzilopochtli, who was in her bosom,
Comforted her, saying:

"Be not afraid,
I know what I must do."

And Coatlicue, having heard
The words of her son,
Was much consoled,
Her heart grew calm,
She felt at peace.

Meanwhile, the four hundred Southerners
met in order to reach an agreement,
And they decided as one
To kill their mother,
For she had defamed them.

They were very angry,
They were very annoyed,
As if their hearts were about to burst from their
  breasts.

Coyolxauhqui incited them greatly,
She fanned the flames of her brothers' ire,
So that they would kill their mother.

And the four hundred Southerners
Made themselves ready,
They attired themselves for war.

Coyolxauhqui, Goddess of the Moon;
Monolithic sculpture of volcanic tufa (225 x
202 x 37 cm). Mexica culture.

122

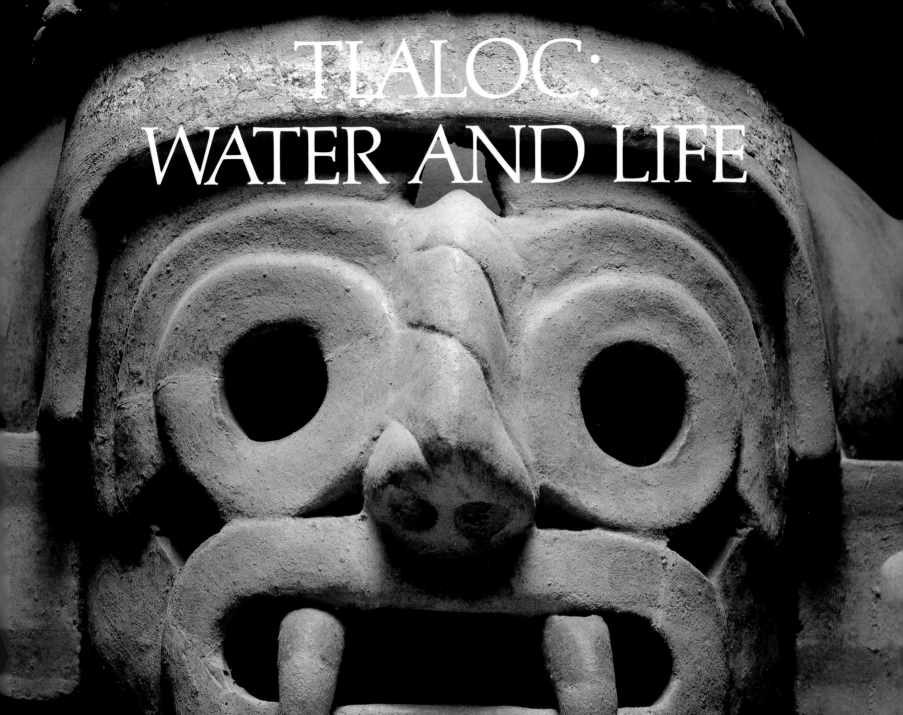

TLALOC:
WATER AND LIFE

As we enter the Hall of Tlaloc, we leave behind the world of war. Here we are received by the god of water, of rain, of fertility. But this god too has his negative side. He visits the earth with hail, frost and all manner of things harmful to crops. He must be appeased, and the entire north side of the Templo Mayor is dedicated to this purpose.

Tlaloc's face is unmistakable: his eyes are two spectacle-like rings. Like his nose, they are made up of snakes. We see him at the entrance to the hall, his forked tongue barely sketched in below the mouth, from which two long fangs protrude. This impressive figure emerges in relief from the lower portion of a blue vase, a form that links the figure immediately with the god's main virtue. Tlaloc is the vessel that waters the earth.

We will see Tlaloc in this guise several times as we tour the Museum of the Templo Mayor. The vase is highly symbolic, as it is a kind of womb which contains the water, the amniotic fluid, that gives rise to life. On the other hand, the vase may also contain the remains of the dead, who thus return to the maternal womb, as in the pot burials recently unearthed at Tlatelolco.

Once again we see the predominance of the color blue on this vase, although the upper portion is also decorated with red. The god's face has black rays and lines. The headdress bears white spikes, and the square earrings include a red and blue pendant.

Actually, two vases with similar characteristics were discovered. The face as it emerges in relief from the ground of the vase wears an intriguing expression. With its great fangs, it is nothing if not imposing. Beneficent or horrific, the character of this deity has been aptly brought to life by the artist in clay, color and form.

Blue vase with Tlaloc mask; Polychromed pottery (34 x 32 cm). Mexica culture.

Zoomorphic miniature representing feline; Green stone (8.5 x 10 cm). Mexica culture.

The offering consists of a box made of *tezontle*, a volcanic rock, with Tlaloc's legs on its sides and two glyphs representing the number thirteen. One glyph seems to represent *quiáhuitl* (rain) and the other *flower* or *cane*. The lid shows the god's face with its two circular eyes and a moustache, under which eight teeth appear, and the hands are situated along the edge of the box. The interior of the box is lined with blue stucco. In it were deposited a quantity of materials, among which the outstanding objects were two large masks from the area of Mezcala, in Guerrero, and a group of serpentine figures.

Group of green stone snakes; *Guerrero area culture.*

Zoomorphic miniature representing lizard; *Green stone (16 x 9 cm). Guerrero area culture.*

Many figures of Tlaloc were unearthed by the excavation, and in addition to figures of the god himself, we have numerous symbols connected with him. One of the collections with the greatest number of such symbols was Offering 41. This offering was found under the platform of Phase IV-B (ca. 1470 A.D.), very near the altar of the frogs that forms part of the platform itself, on the water god's side of the temple.

Also outstanding for their delicacy are a series of small, perfectly formed mother-of-pearl fish, as well as two stone canoes. One of the canoes is of green stone and contains an oar, a propelling device and a harpoon, as well as four mother-of-pearl fish. The other, carved in white stone, also contains an oar.

Group of mother-of-pearl fishes; Mexica culture.

Miniature stone canoes; *Mexica culture.*

Sculpture representing the god Tlaloc; Green stone (31 x 19 x 16 cm). Mexica culture.

One particularly important specimen is a figure of Tlaloc in green stone. This 31-centimeter-tall piece with shell incrustations for eyes was found toward the center of Chamber II, under the stairway that leads to the upper part of the Templo Mayor. That is to say, it is parallel to and contemporaneous with the sculpture of Mayahuel found in Chamber I very near the statue of Coyolxauhqui.

This Tlaloc presided over the offering deposited with him, which consisted of numerous masks from the region of Guerrero. Under it was another alabaster sculpture that has not been fully identified. Both deities are in a squatting position, with Tlaloc's hands embracing his knees. Significantly, a complete cougar's skeleton,

Puma skull with green stone sphere between jaws (9 x 19 x 12.5 cm). Mexica culture.

identified as such by biologists from the Departamento de Prehistoria, was found buried lengthwise along the offering. Its head rested on the green-stone Tlaloc, but as the skin rotted, the cougar's skull rolled away and fell to one side of the god.

In the cougar's jaws was an enormous green stone. We know that when a figure of the nobility died, a jade stone was placed in his mouth. If the dead man were a *macehual*, or commoner, the stone was obsidian. The cougar, deified and associated with Tlaloc, was clearly a significant symbol in this offering.

Mask of the god Tlaloc; *Green stone (16 x 15 x 2 cm). Mexica culture.*

The green Tlaloc is now on display in a glass case along with a diversity of related artifacts, such as other faces and figures of the same god. In the same chamber with Tlaloc were found corals, conchs and a clay vase representing his wife, Chalchiuhtlicue. With her was found a necklace of more than two hundred shell beads which is described in a later chapter.

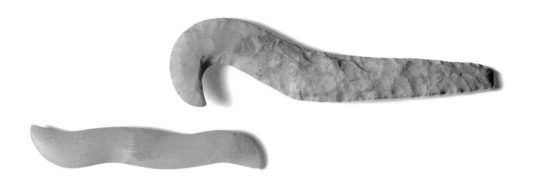

From other offerings dedicated to Tlaloc come such clay artifacts as lightning bolts, spiral forms representing whirlpools and small sculptures painted with Tlaloc's characteristic eyes and moustache. In Offering 18, located on the main facade of the temple at the juncture of the two Phase IV-B buildings, thirteen miniature figures with similar characteristics were discovered. Special mention must be made of a full-body figure of Tlaloc from the Mixteca, in which the rain god's typical features are particularly well-developed within the local style.

And now we come to a work of inconceivable mastery: the stone conch. The author of this sculpture not only brought form to life but also unified mass and rhythm, using incised lines that spread smoothly outward to achieve the eternal motion inherent in this symbol of vitality. In its infinite beauty, the conch reminds us of water, of the sea, of rain, of fertility, of the emergence of other life forms. The conch is the symbol of life par excellence. It lives in the water, it holds life within its shell. It embraces sound, and hence appears in the myth of Quetzalcóatl's descent to Mictlan, the abode of the skeletons, as a dead conch that has fallen silent. He must be bored through by the worms in a sort of sexual act in order to come to life inside once again. Significantly, the remains of conchs and other fresh-water and marine species are the most frequently found artifacts among the offerings of the Templo Mayor.

Stone sculpture of conch (87 x 74 x 44 cm). *Mexica culture.*

Brazier with effigy of Tlaloc; Polychromed stone sculpture (52 x 77 x 39 cm). Mexica culture.

Next we stand before a new face of Tlaloc. This enormous mask formed part of the braziers adorning the temple platform during Phase IV (ca. 1454 A.D.), a period that we have identified with the time of Montezuma I. It was found at the rear of the building on Tlaloc's side of the temple. We have already pointed out that the braziers on Huitzilopochtli's side show a knot of hair tied in a bun and do not wear a face at all. Actually, two monumental Tlaloc masks were found, but one of them was placed on Tlaloc's brazier and can still be seen at its original location. The other is the one we see here in the Museum. Its outstanding features are the ornaments and headdress. On the headdress we see a series of circles inside a band bearing what may be a highly stylized bird on the forehead, all colored red.

On either side of the god's face fall pendants that still preserve the original colors of ocher, blue and red. Emerging from behind the head on either side are pleated paper ornaments beautifully rendered in stone.

Other ornaments in blue adorn this massive sculpture.

Another way of representing the god of water was to show him in the form of a jar. Eleven such sculptures were found within Offering 48, the same offering that contained the remains of infants whose throats had been slit in honor of the rain god.

Child sacrifice was one of the means of honoring Tlaloc, beginning with the month of *Atlcahualo*, when some children were sacrificed at the summit of the mountain bearing Tlaloc's name, while others were cast into the lake and drowned. Offering 48, found on Tlaloc's side of the Templo Mayor, contained the remains of forty-two infants from three to seven years old, above which were placed eleven jars of polychromed stone. The jars bear the familiar features of Tlaloc, with the handle of the jar to the rear. Like the vase, the jar served symbolically to water the earth.

Concerning the association of the children's remains with the offering, it is interesting to note that the period to which they correspond (Phase IV-B, 1470 A.D.), followed a period of great famine in Tenochtitlan due to a prolonged drought with devastating consequences. The connec-

Jar representing the god Tlaloc; Basalt decorated in red, blue, white and black (53 x 32 x 25 cm). Mexica culture.

tion could not be clearer. In this and in numerous other instances, the archeological evidence unearthed at the Templo Mayor dovetailed with the evidence from written historical sources.

In this section of the museum is a plethora of Tlaloc figures. Unlike Huitzilopochtli, whom we see represented almost exclusively in symbols, we see Tlaloc both in symbols and in person. The face of Tlaloc is omnipresent on clay pots and stone pots, in plain or painted pieces. He can be seen in magnificent reliefs, or he may appear scratched into the body of the pot. This repetition of images is a hymn to the survival urge of the Mexicas, who were compelled to maintain the cult of this god whose hands held the water of life. Tlaloc was a powerful spirit who ruled over water in clouds, in the earth, in the sea, in rivers and springs. He had the power to give life or take it away. His presence in the Templo Mayor clearly reflects the way of life of a people who depended on water for their very subsistence.

Vase with mask of Tlaloc in relief; Stone *(23 x 27 cm). Mexica culture.*

Another very important myth is represented on this side of the temple—the myth of *Tonacatépetl*, the mountain of sustenance, where the corn and grains that nourish humans are stored.

In order for nourishment to take place, the gods must intervene. Only through them can created humans succeed in feeding themselves with the primordial grains. The myths speaks to us of how Quetzalcóatl had to go to *Tonacatépetl* to seek the grains that were his gift to humans. Once again we see the sacred mountain which, together with Coatepec, or the serpent's mountain, becomes the dual pyramid that is imbued with the highest degree of holiness. Here, on twin peaks, Tlaloc and Huitzilopochtli dwell side by side.

Vase with mask of Tlaloc; *Pottery (26 x 29 x 26 cm). Mexica culture.*

One of the first stone sculptures uncovered at the temple was a monumental figure of two Tlalocs, one superimposed on the other. This piece gave rise to numerous speculations. In fact, we have yet to resolve the mystery it poses. This enormous block of andesite was broken in several places when it was found, with some of the pieces obviously missing. Nonetheless, the main figure can be clearly seen. It consists of two faces of Tlaloc, one on top of the other. On closer inspection, the figure represents two full-body images of the god, one above the other. The lower figure is formed by currents of water, and the upper body is more representational.

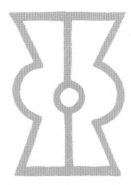

One complication is the appearance on the upper body of breasts, indicating a female figure. The symbol *ollín* (movement) appears on its belly. The general pose of both bodies is similar to that of Tlaltecuhtli, the corpse-devouring earth monster, and the skirt is decorated with human skulls and bones. It is difficult to know exactly what this sculpture represents. Some have speculated that the lower figure represents the earthly water currents, while the upper figure represents the waters of the sky. Others suppose that the sculpture represents the combined presence of Tlaloc and his wife Chalchiuhtlicue. Still others argue that this may represent the sacrifice in honor of Tlaloc in which the priest carried a woman back to back to the heights of the temple, where her throat was slit. All we can say with certainty is that symbolism is the mysterious nexus of this art that expresses myth and symbol in the power of stone, color and form.

Sculpture of the gods Tlaltecuhtli and Tlaloc; Stone (122 x 97 x 33 cm). Mexica culture.

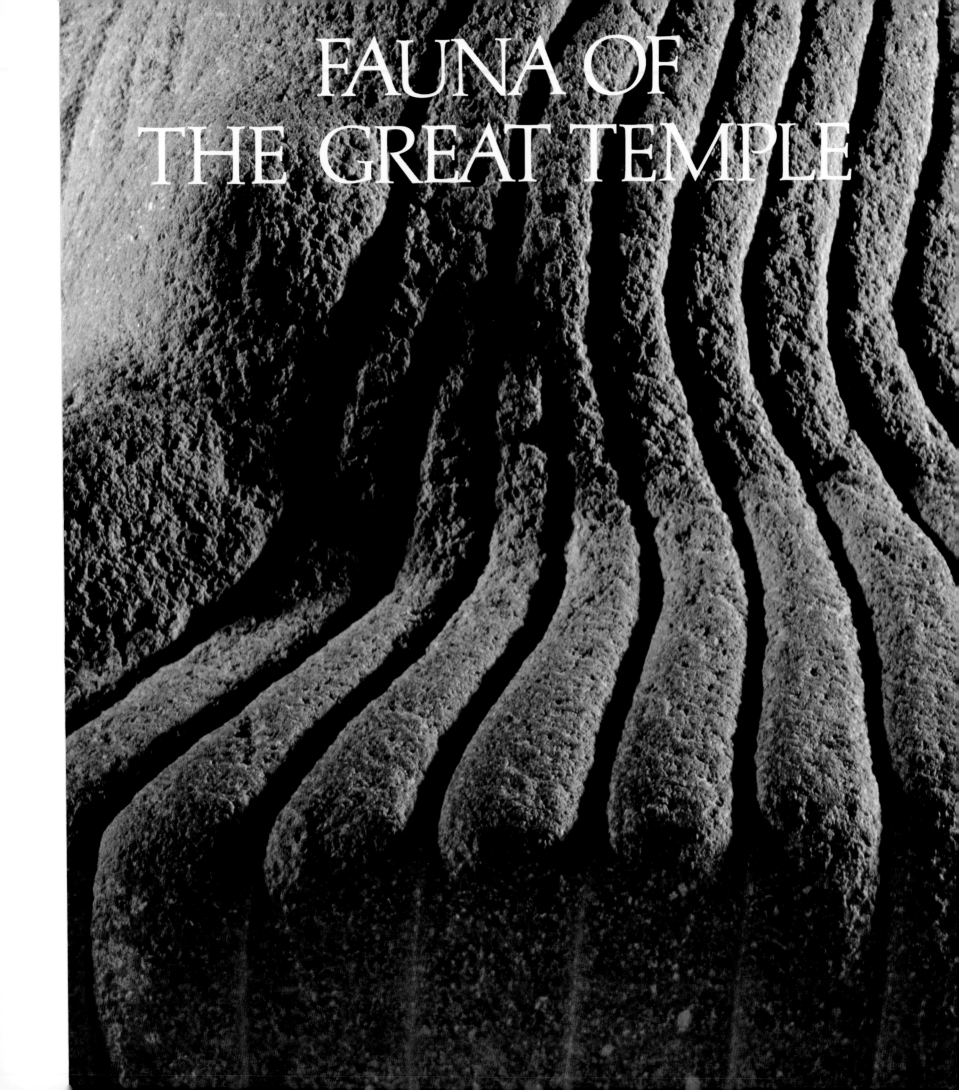

FAUNA OF
THE GREAT TEMPLE

Turtle shells; *Basalt, green stone and shell. Mexica culture.*

Group of fishes; *Green stone and mother-of-pearl. Mexica culture.*

One piece particularly outstanding for its workmanship is a stone eagle's head that still retains some of its original coloring. It was found in the same offering as the turtle, in the interior of the Red Temple, on the south side of the ceremonial complex.

This remarkable work recalls the eagle's role as the symbol of Huitzilopochtli and hence of the sun. Sheaves which appear to represent locks of hair hang from either side of the eagle's head in a style characteristic of a warrior's headdress.

Next on our tour is a white clay brazier remarkable for the enormous face of Tlaloc that covers almost the entire body of the piece. Although it immediately suggests the rain god's familiar face, this representation is unique in certain respects. There is an abundance of built-up elements. The two eyes have large, bulky lids, and tears gush from them and flow down the cheeks. The nose is given a unique appearance by the extra elements attached to it. Tlaloc's forked tongue emerges from the mouth. Eight braziers like this one were found placed in pairs facing the salients, or altars, in the Hall of the Eagle Warriors, and it is clear that they were designed for burning copal during certain ceremonies.

Eagle head; Stone with red, black and green pigment (25.5 x 13 cm). Mexica culture.

Brazier with representation of the face of Tlaloc; Pottery (62.5 x 51 cm). Mexica culture.

152

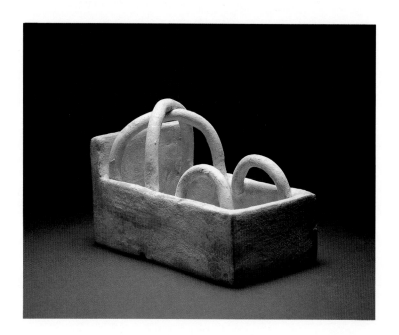

Miniature cradle; *Pottery (15 x 9 cm).*
Mexica culture.

Various offerings contained a number of small clay cradles, with their obvious connection to birth and life. From birth, an individual could be associated with a particular animal or object, depending on the day and hour in which he was born. Hence the importance of animals and their relationship to a person throughout his life.

Also significant is the role played by music in a series of rituals that marked passages from birth to death. Many musical instruments were found in the offerings, some of them actual instruments, while others are sculptural representations of instruments. Different types of flutes, timbrels, small drums, *teponaztles*, *caparachos* and conchs were found. The number and variety of this type of artifact says a great deal about the importance of music in the daily life of the Mexicas.

Clay flute with face; *Polychromed pottery in blue and red (16 x 4 cm). Mexica culture.*

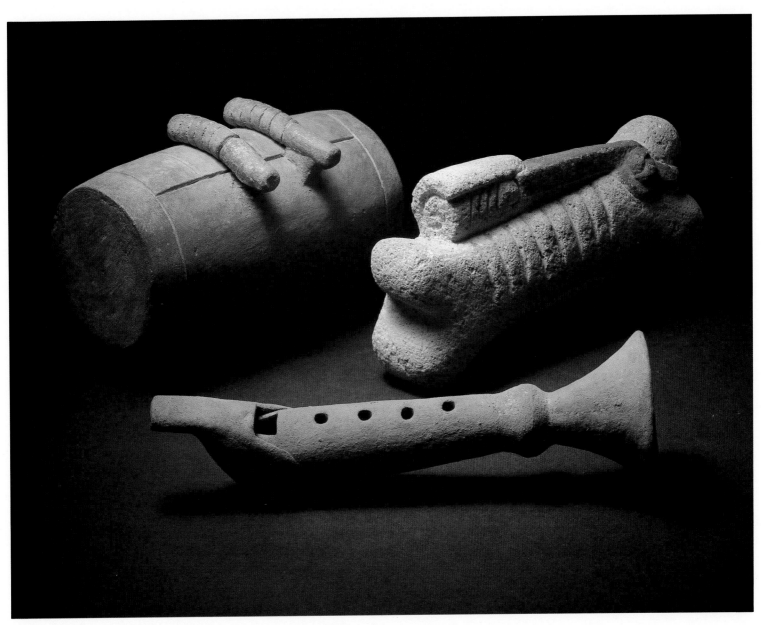

Representations of musical instruments; *Pottery and stone. Mexica culture.*

The link between images of the gods of water and various types of fauna grows stronger when we look at the objects discovered in Chamber III on Tlaloc's side of the temple. One cache consisted of two richly polychromed vases between which rested the bony remains of a jaguar with a flint knife in its jaws. Close inspection of one vase reveals that one side is painted in vivid colors with an image of Chalchiuhtlicue, goddess of water and wife of Tlaloc. The face and feet emerge in relief from the body of the pot, and her attire is distinctively drawn.

On the other side is a representation of Tlaloc with his long fangs. Of particular interest is the lid that covered the mouth of the pot, a kind of decorated plate with predominantly orange coloring. On it we see Tlaloc painted once again. He is shown as he is found sometimes in the codices, with his arms extended forward, slinging water from a pot. Beneath the lid was a mask from the area of Guerrero, and the interior of the pot contained more than three thousand green stone beads.

The coloring of this piece is impressive, and it is worth noting that this specimen was found in perfect condition. The position of the jaguar between the two polychromed jars testifies to its particular significance to Tlaloc and his cult.

Stone beads; Mexica culture.

Cholula-style vase with two faces, one of the god Tlaloc and one of fertility goddess; Polychromed clay (47 x 34 cm). Mixteca culture.

Other pieces are thought to be related to particular rites, such as the two clay braziers bearing the figure of an unknown deity. One of them was found to contain a quantity of copal that still retained its original color. This god's accessories include a headdress with a number of peaks and the pleated paper ornament characteristic of certain gods appears behind his head. He is wearing a necklace with tubular beads and several flowers adorn his chest. Some of these ornaments would lead one to postulate a relationship with the water divinities.

Ceremonial urn with figure of deity, (front and side views); Pottery (24 x 23 cm). Mexica culture.

A dark brown vase representing Chalchiuhtlicue, wife of Tlaloc, was found in Chamber II, as mentioned earlier. Like the related polychrome figure from Chamber III, the face and feet of this Chalchiuhtlicue, as well as the pleated paper ornament behind her head, stand out from the

*Vase representing the goddess Chalchiuhtlicue, (front and side views); **Pottery (33 x 33 cm). Mexica culture.***

body of the vase. She bears two concentric circles on her chest, which may indicate a breastplate or chest pendant of some sort. This vase was found in a prominent position at the entrance to the chamber, accompanied by conchs and to one side of some marine corals.

Let us now examine another vase of superior workmanship inscribed with a majestic face of Tlaloc. The predominantly blue and white colors are outlined by the incised lines that define the various elements of the god's face and headdress. The long eyebrows culminating in the twisted nose, the eye-rings and the mouth with its prominent fangs, in addition to the forked tongue barely suggested below the mouth, make this one of the most powerful of the many images of Tlaloc. Inside the vase were found snail shells which, together with the vase itself, formed part of Offering 31. This piece was of course found on Tlaloc's side of the temple.

Vase with figure of Tlaloc; Polychromed pottery (30 x 31 cm). Mexica culture.

One can hardly discuss the gods and animals related to water and fertility without including the head of *Xipe-Totec* found at the site in a colonial well, among sheep's horns and pottery of European make. How the head came to rest in the well is not known. Nonetheless, the connection between this god and the spring rites of renewal is worthy of note. *Xipe* is usually represented dressed in the skin of a sacrificial victim, and in fact this is how he appears in this figure. The cord that binds and stretches the skin of the victim and the double mouth on the face call to mind the fertility rituals in which the priest attired himself in the skin of the flayed victim. The expression on the face speaks for itself. Once again death is the form that gives new life, in the endless cycle of sacrifice so prevalent in prehispanic Mexico.

Xipe-Totec, god of the silver-smiths; Stone head (13 x 12 cm). Mexica culture.

We now come to two pieces whose significance is self-evident in this world where symbol and myth are transformed into esthetic values: an enormous necklace of mother-of-pearl and shell, and an alabaster deer.

The necklace was found in Chamber II encircling the sculpture of Tlaloc in green stone. It contains more than two hundred repeating figures. Among them is a serpent's head and rattle, as well as frogs, snails and fish.

A number of gold beads also form part of the necklace, and a figure of a frog in green stone serves as its central pendant. Its importance within the offering where it was found is indicated by the fact that it adorned the figure of the presiding god, Tlaloc. The material from which the figures have been carved—shell—could not be more significant. Here is an ornament worthy of a god indeed. In this truly impressive piece, each of the aquatic and terrestrial animals that comprise it is highly evocative.

Necklace, (detail and complete view); Mother-of-pearl, green stone and gold; Mexica culture.

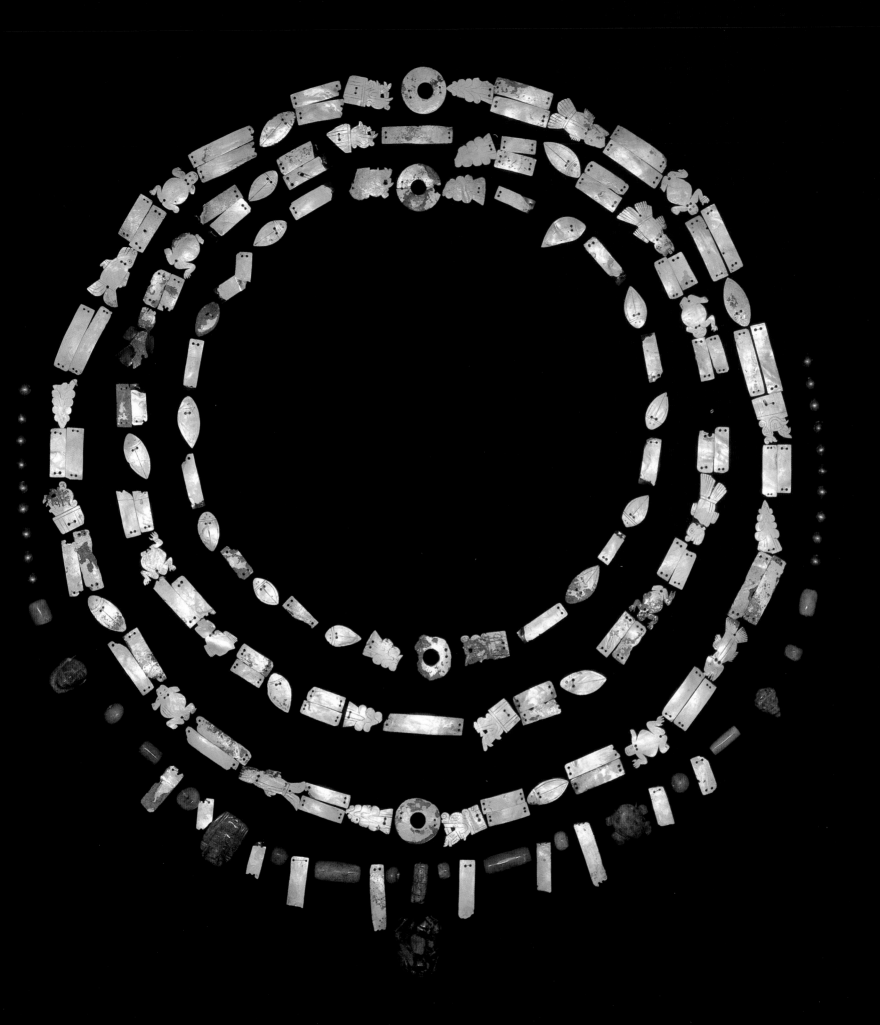

Deer head; *Alabaster (10 cm). Mexica culture.*

The second piece is an extraordinarily delicate alabaster deer's head with a long, graceful neck. This piece was found together with two other figures carved from the same material—a dart and another piece identified as

Deer head; *Green stone (10 cm). Mexica culture.*

a cloud. These three elements appear
to be associated with one another
wherever they are found; on numerous occasions we unearthed similar
ensembles not only in alabaster, but
also in clay and even stone.

Unfortunately, we can say little about the significance of the association of these three forms. We can only hope that studies now underway will help clarify the relationship between them. In the meantime, we cannot fail to admire the artistry of the craftsman whose hands, working without metal tools, so ably captured the dignity and delicacy of the deer that it still touches us five hundred years after its creation.

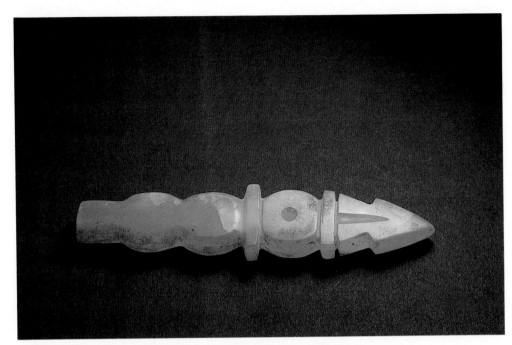

Miniature representing solar dart; Alabaster (12.2 cm). Mexica culture.

In these halls, we have not only met the rain god face to face, but we have seen him present in his symbols. His cult is also expressed in flowers, song and poetry. Here is a hymn in his honor, in which the singer asks for a loan from the god and the moment comes when the god sends water to the earth by shedding tears:

Oh, in Mexico they are asking to
*   borrow from the god.*
There, where the paper flags are flying,
*   and all along the four directions,*
*   men are standing.*
At last the time for his weeping has
*   come!*

Ah, I was created and I bring festive
*   bundles of bloody stalks to the sacred*
*   patio of my god.*
Ah, you are my leader, Oh Wizard
*   Prince,*
*   and though truly you produced*
*   your corn, our nourishment,*
*   though you are first among all, they*
*   only bring you shame.*
Ah, but if anyone brings me
*   shame,*
*   it is because he did not know me*
*   well:*
*   you, on the other hand, are my*
*   fathers,*
*   my priesthood, Serpent-Tiger . . .*
Ah, from Tlalocan, in a turquoise
*   ship,*
*   Acatónal has departed, to be seen*
*   no more. . .*

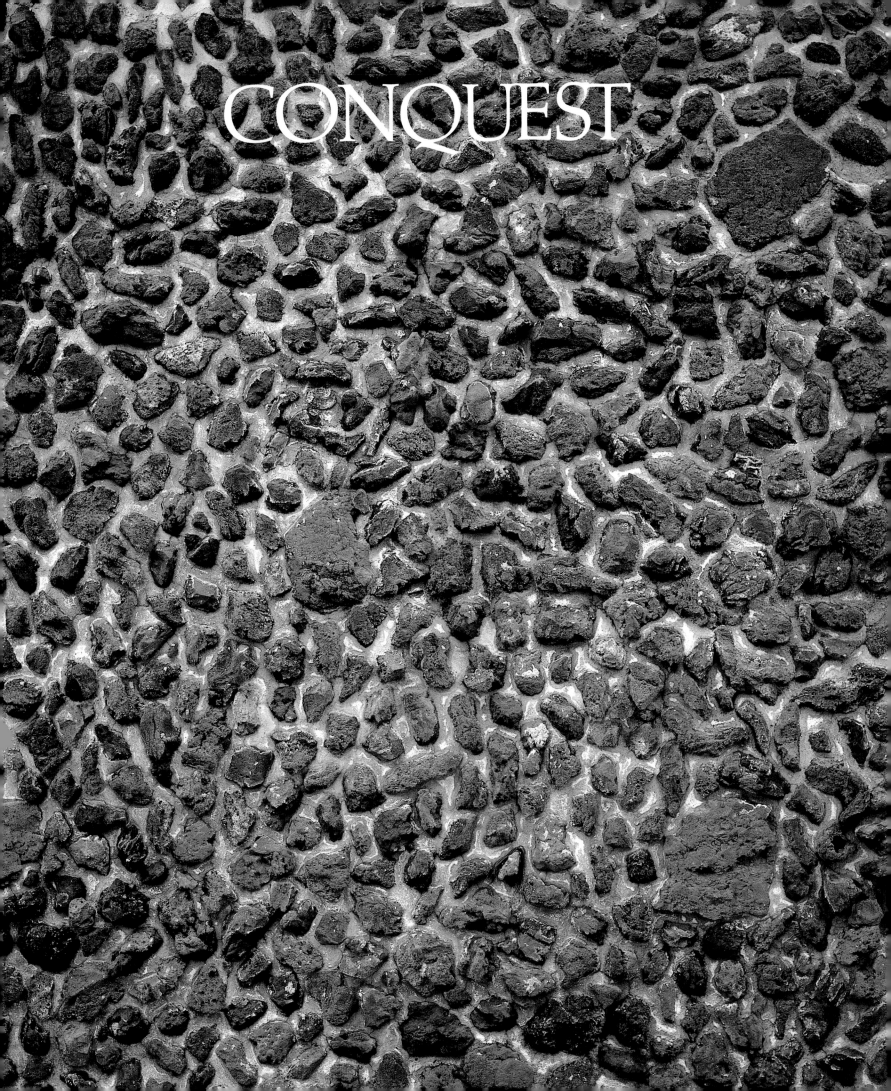

CONQUEST

Jesuit coat-of-arms; Stone (45 x 36 cm). Colonial.

The last hall of the Museum is dedicated to the Conquest. With the arrival of the Spaniards, two phases of conquest began: military and ideological. The triumph of Spanish arms over the Mexicas on August 13, 1521, merely continued the spiritual conquest that was already underway.

And what became of the Templo Mayor? Like all the other buildings in the main ceremonial complex, it was destroyed. The vestiges we have found correspond to earlier periods, and represent the smaller artifacts that were less likely to be broken up and obliterated. On the very site of the great *Teocalli*, or Temple, the conquerors built their homes. Not one visible trace was left of the Templo Mayor complex, a fact that gave rise to a great deal of speculation. The conquerors' wish was fulfilled: nothing visible remained of the Indian's culture and that which he considered the center of his universe, the Navel of the World.

In addition to Aztec artifacts, the excavation of the temple yielded vestiges of the colonial world from Spanish buildings located on the site of the Templo Mayor. Bases of colonial columns, on whose lower portion more than once appeared the image of the god Tlaltecuhtli, were recovered. Pottery, capitals of columns and other artifacts were also found. Of particular interest were the stone coats-of-arms that must certainly have belonged to the Jesuits who dwelled on this historic site for some three hundred years.

Remains of prehispanic objects that may have been partially destroyed in the sixteenth century also came to light. We know that many sculptures were put to new use as columns, millstones and other useful objects. During the course of the excavation, fragments of a statue of Coyolxauhqui were uncovered that we know, because of their location, represent a later construction phase than any of those described in the preceding pages. That is to say, they must have been a part of very recent phases of the temple. In short, in spite of their brutal thoroughness, the temple's destroyers were unable completely to obliterate this world that refused to die, that remained latent, waiting for more than five hundred years to be salvaged from beneath the layer of concrete on which the modern city of Mexico rests.

Since the excavation of the Templo Mayor, numerous cultural artifacts have continued to emerge from various locations around the city. One recent find was an enormous sculpture of Tlaltecuhtli under the Paseo de la Reforma, near the Museum of Anthropology, with a hole in the middle of the sculpture indicating that the Spaniards had put it to use as a millstone.

Colonial column cut from Mexica representation of the god Tlaltecuhtli; Stone (59 x 70 x 67 cm).

More recently —on Monday, July 4, 1988— news went out of the discovery by Salvamento Arqueológico del Instituto Nacional de Antropología e Historia (Office of Archeological Salvage of the National Institute of Anthropology and History) of a monumental circular sculpture similar to the Stone of Tizoc, with sun's rays around the upper half. This stone block contains sculpted figures of Huitzilopocthli conquering his enemies. Interestingly, the figure was found at the Ex-arzobispado (the Former Seat of the Archbishopric) at the corner of Moneda and Licenciado Verdad streets. Here the majestic temple of Tezcatlipoca once stood. One can still see, along Moneda street, the elevation caused by the

underground remains of this important building. The image on the stone clearly reveals Huitzilopochtli as the blue Tezcatlipoca who rules the southern quadrant of the universe.

Hopefully this piece will remain where it was found; its removal to a museum would take it out of context. The time has come when artifacts such as these should remain at the site of discovery—in this case, the side patio of the colonial building located at the site. The locale is well-suited to the piece; visitors can view it in a setting that clearly relates two great monuments of our history.

Two streams converge to form the character of the Mexican people: the cultures of prehispanic Mexico and of colonial Mexico. One sought unsuccessfully to deny the other, but images of the former continue to emerge from under the earth, making its presence felt again and again.

These are the gods who refuse to die.

MAP OF ARCHEOLOGICAL SITE

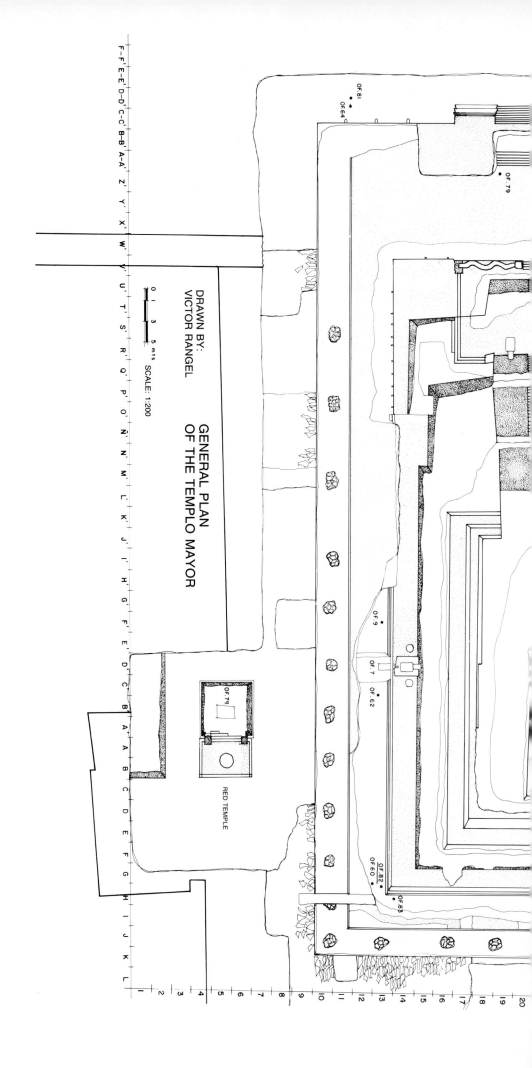

GENERAL PLAN
OF THE TEMPLO MAYOR

DRAWN BY:
VICTOR RANGEL

SCALE: 1:200

RED TEMPLE

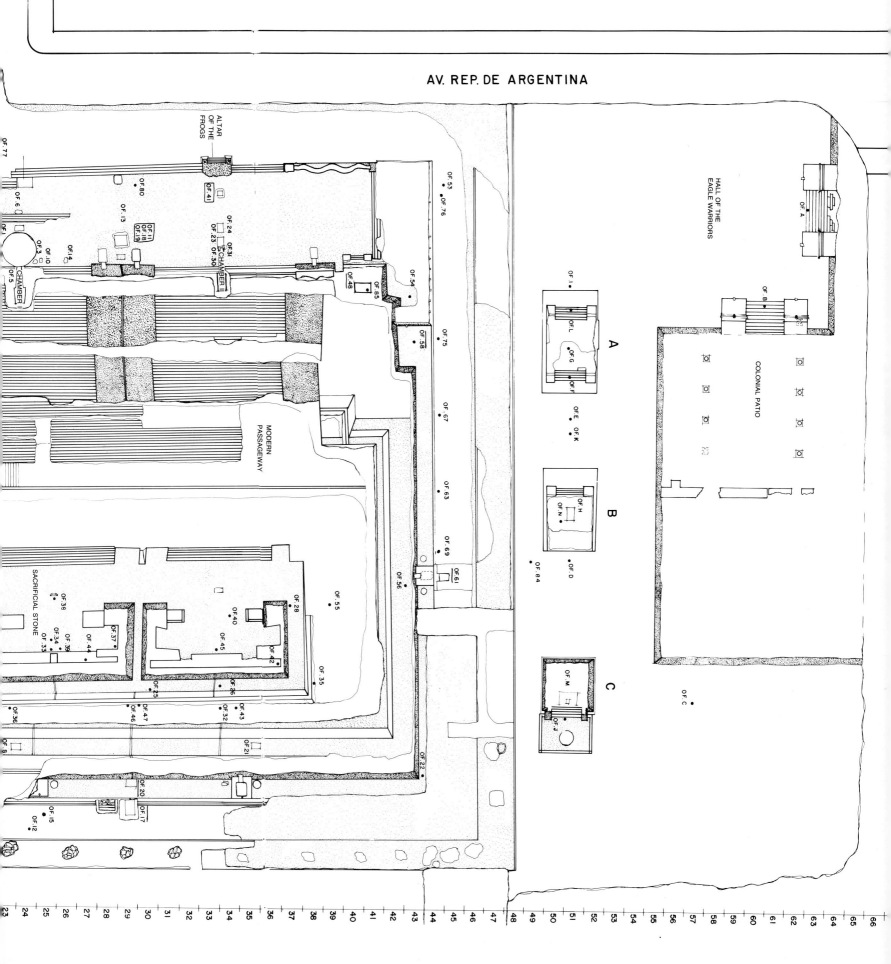

AV. REP. DE ARGENTINA

ANNOTATED BIBLIOGRAPHY

The works to which we have referred in the text are basic to an understanding of Mexica society. Among the chroniclers is Fray Bernardino de Sahagún with his monumental work *Historia de las cosas de la Nueva España* (History of New Spain's Affairs), which has appeared in a number of editions in Spanish as well as other languages. Fray Diego Durán and Motolinía are two other colonial chroniclers who have left us a wealth of information in their respective works *Historia de las Indias de Nueva España* (History of the Indies of New Spain) and *Memoriales* (Memoranda). The same is true of authors like Hernando Alvarado Tezozomoc with his *Crónica mexicana* (Mexican Chronicle), and of course, the *Historia verdadera de la conquista de la Nueva España* (A True History of the Conquest of New Spain) by Bernal Díaz del Castillo, and Hernán Cortés's *Cartas de relación* (Informative Letters) to the king of Spain. All of these works give facts of great interest for a knowledge of the Mexicas in general and of the Templo Mayor in particular.

Also essential are a number of modern works, such as Dr. Miguel León Portilla's well-known works *Filosofía Náhuatl* (Nahuatl Philosophy) and *Los Antiguos Mexicanos* (The Ancient Mexicans), as well as an important work from the pen of Alfredo López Austin, *Cuerpo Humano e Ideología* (Ideology and the Human Body). Another essential reference is *Economía Política e Ideología en el México Prehispánico* (Economy and Ideology in Prehispanic Mexico), coordinated by Pedro Carrasco and Johanna Broda, the fourth edition of which was published by Editorial Nueva Imagen in 1985.

A great many articles, books, exhibit catalogs, conference proceedings—in fact more than a hundred titles in several languages—have appeared on the topic of the Templo Mayor since its excavation.